From Your Biggest Fan

Discovering the Potential
of Those We Love and Lead

Jason Patterson

Published in the United States by Threeleaf Publishing LLC.

ISBN 978-1-957690-03-2

Subjects: Religion—Christian Living—Inspirational

First Edition

Cover design by Todd Neilson

For Andrea

Table of Contents

Foreword by Bob Goff

I've never been one for titles, though I've had a few along the way, like *lawyer, diplomat,* and *entrepreneur.* Unfortunately, those weren't getting me invited to as many parties as I'd like, so I summarized them into *Chief of Fun and Whimsy.* Not long ago, I boiled it down to *Chief Balloon Inflator* because every shindig needs one of those. What I've been learning is titles don't mean as much as we might imagine. The truth is, we already have the best one we'll ever get: *friend.* It's not only the one Jesus gave us; it's the one that guarantees we'll be invited to celebrate with those we love.

That's my kind of title.

Having the chance to be friends with someone means a lot of beautiful things. One of them is that we have a little bit of influence with them. We might have other titles in people's lives that give us some clout, like boss, coach, or dad. Whatever the reason, we've all got influence with someone. The question is how well are we using it?

There's incredible potential in everyone. Jesus is the one who put it there. That's why it's worth rethinking how well we're helping others to discover it. If we will, every day can become like a party because we're championing the potential in others and celebrating them—not so much for what they've accomplished, but for who they're becoming. That doesn't mean it will be easy or that we won't have tough conversations as we speak the truth in love. It will just be worth it.

The message of this book is powerful not only because it can make our lives better, but because it can change the lives of those we love most. Its message isn't just one we need to hear. It's the one our kids and spouses need us to grasp. The lives of our neighbors, co-workers, and friends will be better if we use our influence to help them discover who Jesus made them to be.

Jason wrote *From Your Biggest Fan* because he's convinced being the champion of everyone around you is the most enjoyable way to live and lead. It helps us to focus on others the way Jesus did and be more mindful of the wonder He has woven into each of us.

Jason is calling us to be each other's biggest fans. I'm one of his, and yours too.

Becoming the champion of those we love is a journey worth taking. I'm in the crowd of people cheering you on. Look for me; I'll be the one handing out balloons.

—*Bob*

Author's Note

This is a book about leadership, but not organizational leadership. John Maxwell and Patrick Lencioni have that category locked down anyway. This is about what we might call relational leadership. It's about the influence we all have in the lives of others and learning how to deploy it using the selfless life of Jesus as a model. He is the first and last "biggest fan leader" and our ultimate example. This book offers a mindset for leadership that can be applied within any model or organization whether you're at home or in the office, in an entry level position or at the top. It's inclusive and simple, and therefore deceptively powerful.

The longer I live the more passionate I become about helping others discover who God truly made them to be. I hope you fall in love with the beauty of uncovering the hidden wonder in those around you. As you do, you'll also wind up realizing who you are in profound, beautiful, and surprising ways because God works through the principle of sowing and reaping. What you do for others, God will do for you.

For readers whose faith in Jesus is the center of their lives, the biblical underpinning for the mindset this book argues we adopt is Ephesians 2:10 (my life verse!). Our focus in the pages ahead is *only* the first sentence of that verse, which is set up in the first chapter. Everything that follows is how we must live and lead if we want to help others discover the truth of what God says about us in this powerful scripture. While it's not the subject of this book, the rest of what is taught in Ephesians 2:10 is *vitally important* for a full understanding of the truth, and is thoroughly treated in the Bible study that accompanies this book.

This book isn't just about what I believe; it's my own journey as well. I chose to write the book this way because I feel my struggles with insecurity and negativity, among other things, would help better serve you as the reader. My desire is for you to find freedom knowing we're all on the same journey and experience renewed hope that you can overcome the obstacles in your path as well.

You'll find several people throughout the book who inspired me to champion others better. Primarily my wife's grandpa, David Mainse, who was my hero. In many ways, this book is an act of love for him. He was very well-known among his own generation and throughout his home country of Canada, but most people today have never heard of him. I wrote this book to honor how he inspired me to live and lead, and to share him with the world. If you google his name, you'll find endless videos of his television programming. It's outdated now and will come across as a bit cheesy at times, but he was the most incredible leader, genuine Christian, and loving family man I have ever known. I hope you enjoy meeting him in the pages that follow.

The Bible study, along with other resources to help you champion others, are available at biggestfanleaders.com.

Welcome to the journey of becoming the biggest fan of those you love and lead! I'm so glad to be on it together.

—*Jason*

PART I

A New Mindset

"[T]hose who cannot change their minds cannot change anything."[1]

George Bernard Shaw

1

The Fastest Man Alive

GROWING UP, LOUIE ZAMPERINI LACKED everything but trouble. He was born in 1917 into a poor family of Italian immigrants. Before his third birthday his parents packed up their few possessions and moved to the dry climate of Torrance, California. Louie would become infamous running the streets of that town, usually to avoid getting caught after stealing food, or some other kind of mischief. Eventually, Louie's speed would find its way to the track and carry him to a fame no one could have imagined.

Near the end of eighth grade, Louie was in a pinch yet again, this time for breaking into the gym at Torrance High, earning him a ban from school athletics and social activities from the principal. Louie's older brother Pete stepped in. He argued Louie could change if he could compete—he only needed the chance to succeed. After a bit of wrangling, the principal relented and Louie was made eligible to run track the following semester.[1] Louie didn't know it yet, but in his brother, he now possessed the secret to success:

Someone who could see his true potential.

In his first race, Louie lumbered across the finish line out of breath and in last place. He darted under the bleachers to hide, humiliated. Things couldn't have gone worse in Louie's mind, but that day, Pete's spine was steeled; Louie would succeed. No matter what it took.

After that loss, Pete began riding his bike behind Louie to help him keep pace while training, swiping at him with a stick when he slowed. Louie hated every minute of it, but Pete got him to keep racing, physically dragging him to his second meet, and soon enough, Louie started to win—*a lot.*

In the fall of that year, Pete traveled back from his nearby junior college to train Louie almost every day. By this time, Louie was a more willing student, and progress came fast. Wearing black silk shorts his mother made for him out of a skirt, Louie broke the school record for the 880-meter race. If you're ever caught wearing silk shorts your mom made for you, break a record of some kind. It will keep people's minds off the shorts.

In his first mile long race, Louie broke Pete's record by three seconds. He finished the season undefeated. Soon after, at a statewide meet at UCLA, the crowd was shocked when Louie won by over a quarter of a mile. The competition wasn't even in sight.

Only two years later, Louie beat a field of runners believed to be the best in history and broke a national high school record by over two seconds. In two more years, he fulfilled a dream and qualified for the Olympics to be held in Germany. Mercifully, uniforms were provided, and Louie could retire his homemade shorts for good. At the games in Berlin, Louie set a world record for the fastest lap ever run in the 5000-meter race. Every victory was proof that Pete was right; Louie was special.

During his race in the 1938 NCAA National Championships, a group of competitors tried to sabotage Louie mid-race. In their planned attack, a group of runners surrounded Louie and began to stomp his feet and slash his shins with the spikes of their track shoes that had been illegally sharpened before the race. During the scuffle a well-placed elbow broke Louie's rib. At the final turn, Louie found a gap, and broke through the group. He shot past the leader, crossing the finish line in first place with blood gushing from his shins and a searing pain in his chest. The crowd gasped and Louie was stunned when the results appeared on the board. He had run the fastest mile in NCAA history and was 1.9 seconds shy of running the fastest mile in human history.

Louie's achievements on the track are mind-blowing, but they aren't the most incredible or inspiring parts of his story. For that, we have to go back to Louie's earliest years before the family's move to Torrance.[2]

Wonders Waiting

In 1919, two-year-old Louie came down with double pneumonia. The family doctor advised a move to a drier climate, so Louie's parents made the move to California. Despite their efforts, throughout his first years there his lungs had not returned to full capacity. Louie couldn't keep up with the other kids, and every girl and boy in town left him in their dust.[3]

The fastest man alive was once the slowest kid in town.

As a young boy, Louie's God-given potential was invisible. When he was hopelessly slow and losing every footrace, his ability to be a world-class track athlete, compete at the highest levels, and shatter world records was already in him. The problem was no one could see it; especially Louie.

Not a single person came up to little dust-covered Louie, patted him on the head, and told him, "Don't worry, someday you'll be the fastest man on the planet." No one said it because no one could see it.

There is unseen God-given potential in every person, longing to be discovered. That belief is why I wrote this book. What remains unseen in people remains unfulfilled. That breaks my heart. I imagine it breaks God's too.

I want to offer a new mindset, a new way of thinking that will help you discover and fulfill the hidden potential in those you love and lead. My hope is that this book will inspire you to devote your life to helping others see who they truly are. There are big hurdles we'll have to jump to get there. I've stumbled over them all. We'll look at each of them on this journey and set out some simple habits we can develop that will help us dig for the treasure within the people around us.

There are people in your life right now who look like the slowest kid in town but are capable of a superhuman speed of their own. Like Louie in his early life, they just don't know it yet. There is incredible potential in our kids waiting to be unearthed. There is greatness in our co-workers in the next cubicle over. Wonders are waiting in every person.

The world is already full of people like Louie, but it desperately needs more people like Pete. People ready to pick up the necessary tools and help those around them become all God created them to be.

Skyglow and Supernovas

To a junior high student, any taste of freedom is sweet. My first late-night swim in a friend's backyard pool felt like a rite of passage. After a long stretch of random conversations about how much money we'd like to make some day and pranks we'd like to pull on our friends, we reached a lull and began looking up at the stars. That's when I became convinced I saw something incredible. I thought I saw a star disappear.

For the record, I did not. Stars don't just quit glowing when they die—they supernova. But my 14-year-old brain didn't know that at the time. There is actually a star visible in the night sky today scientists believe could die any moment. It's a red supergiant at the shoulder of the Orion constellation with a radius over 900 times that of our sun. When it goes supernova, it will swell to 7,000 times its current luminosity and shine for a short period with the brightness of 10 billion suns put together. Feel free to read that sentence again.

Not a bad way to go if you're a star.[4]

That night I experienced a fleeting sense of awe based on something that turned out to be a hallucination (I did not see a star disappear), but my friends and I should have experienced a lasting sense of wonder with an unobstructed view of the billions of stars stretched across the Milky Way. The problem is we couldn't see most of our galaxy's stars—even on a clear night—due to a phenomenon of the modern world called skyglow. Skyglow is the result of light pollution caused by billboards, neon signs, headlights, streetlights, and even the lamplight spilling out of our windows around us. It robs us of the ability to see the heavens as they truly are.

There is a well-known set of side-by-side photos, both taken by Todd Carlson, on the night of the Northeast Blackout—a massive power outage affecting 55 million people in Canada and the U.S. In his picture taken on an ordinary evening before the blackout, almost no stars can be seen above the house in the foreground, even though it's a clear night. Todd's picture taken from the same vantage point the night of the blackout is awe-inspiring. With the effects of light pollution removed, the sky is bursting with colors and stars.[5]

I wonder what it would be like to see side-by-side pictures of everyone around us—one as we see them, the other as God sees them. If something like that were available during Louie's early years, the first picture would have been of a misfit boy with no future. The second would be of a champion capable of nearly superhuman speed, not to mention the ability to inspire millions of people. No one but Pete had ever even caught a glimpse of that second picture. Worse yet, Louie had never seen it either.

Without Pete, Louie would have never set world records as an Olympian, or been considered the fastest person on earth. Louie needed his older brother. He needed someone to help him see his potential. There are people all around us that need someone to be Pete in their lives too.

I believe that person is you.

Pete used a bicycle and a stick to drive Louie out of his complacency. When we champion people in our lives, the tools we use might be different. One thing is sure; we'll need Pete's grit. You can check the label sometime for yourself, but I'm pretty sure grit is the first ingredient in greatness. Pete had it in spades. Because of Pete, soon Louie would as well.

Because of you, those you love and lead can too.

Being a former track coach who had trained a string of winners over a long career wasn't on Pete's resume. No one under his tutelage had ever become an Olympian. You and I don't have to be any of those things either. All Pete possessed was a clear view of the wonders waiting in his little brother, the grit and determination to turn him into a champion, and a mountain of grace for his hardheaded sibling. What we need is a new mindset, allowing us to better see those we love and lead as God truly made them to be.

Masterpiece

There was once a tentmaker named Paul with an active mind. While he was making his tents, Paul thought a lot about the God of creation. It led him to write some incredible things. It's likely no one realized it then, but Paul would go on to become one of the best-selling authors of all time and one of the most quoted people in history. Whatever Paul's contemporaries thought of him, I would venture a guess no one envisioned that kind of success. (No one but God. God intimately knows the wonders he wove into every one of us.)

Paul used his writing to help people understand themselves and God better. Of all the things he wrote, one of my favorites is a line in a short letter to some people he deeply loved and believed in. Paul told them they are each God's masterpiece.[6] Let that sink in for a moment. You are God's *masterpiece*. You are the handiwork of the Master of all craftsman. That truth is the foundation for the mindset needed to discover the greatness in others.

It's not enough for us to simply know we are God's masterpiece. We need to be able to see it in ourselves. The problem is we're all too close to the painting. When we look at ourselves it's like looking at a ten-foot-wide painting from three inches away. It's our own form of skyglow—we just cannot see the full beauty of our God-given potential. That's why Pete could see what Louie could not.

Louie deserved to have Pete in his corner. Those around us deserve someone in theirs who will believe in them, and fight to help them uncover their unseen potential. We can become their secret to success.

If you've had someone like Pete in your life, you know how powerful it is to be believed in. If you haven't, you have the power to make sure others won't repeat that part of your story.

We all know people like Louie, who are hiding under the bleachers in humiliation and defeat. Don't let them stay there. Pick them up, dust them off, and drive them toward fulfilling the good things God has planned for them. Like Pete, drag them if you have to. Whether they're in your family, your classroom, or are a member of your staff, they are worth your best. Love and lead them with grit and grace. Get in their corner and remain there until they can see themselves the way God created them to be.

2

The Ripple Effect

IN AUGUST OF 1772, A killer hurricane rolled across the island of St. Croix. While others were picking up the pieces of broken buildings, seventeen-year-old Alexander Hamilton decided to write an account of the storm for a local publication. His evocative account of the storm would become his ticket to a new life.

It was a life that never should have happened. Hamilton was an illegitimate child, a significant setback in society then. He was abandoned by his father at eleven. After his mother died at thirteen, he was sent to live with a first cousin who committed suicide within a year. Hamilton experienced the pain of abandonment, the fear of uncertainly, and the trauma of death at every turn. The odds of succeeding in life were heavily stacked against him. In that day, climbing the ladder of success would have been unlikely for Hamilton, no matter how brilliant or capable he was. Leaving the island and being educated in a prestigious college would have been impossible for someone of Hamilton's pedigree.

Yet, that's exactly what happened. Hamilton's life was changed forever when a group of strangers lifted him out of obscurity through their generosity. When Hamilton's stirring account of the hurricane was published, his talent was obvious. Hamilton's brilliant mind wasn't difficult to spot in his writing. He had flare. What's most impressive is not that his abilities were noticed—perhaps they weren't buried as deep as Louie's, or mine or yours—it's that a group of admirers *did something about it.* In light of his talent, a small band of merchants assembled to take up a collection to pay for Hamilton's education in North America. They weren't his relatives, his employers, or even his friends, but they saw something unique in him and bet part of their fortunes on his future. No one could have imagined what was to come.

Within five years after arriving in New York, Hamilton graduated from King's College, was hired to be George Washington's chief of staff during the Revolution, and became a war hero after leading a daring charge in the battle at Lexington. Hamilton was a major player in writing the Constitution and helped propel it to ratification with his essays in the Federalist Papers. Appointed by Washington as the first U.S. Treasury Secretary, Hamilton was able to shape America into the country we know today. The ripple effects of the people that bankrolled Hamilton's future are still impacting our lives and economy in profound ways to this day.[1]

Every opportunity to invest in someone's life and future is as unique as that person. God places people in front of us and asks that we believe in them. Who they become and what they accomplish isn't up to us. Most won't become Olympians or towering historical figures with a statue in Washington, D.C. But that doesn't matter. We are not in charge of what others do with the opportunities we give them. We only control whether or not we afford them with one.

If they go on to become a better parent, a more generous employer, or a kinder neighbor, it will be worth whatever we contributed to their lives. As we invest in the lives of those we love and lead there will be a ripple effect. We're not in charge of how tall the waves are or how far they reach. That's God's responsibility. Ours is the same as the unlikely group of people who placed their bet on a socially unacceptable teenager—to see the potential in God's people and *do something about it.*

I Don't Care If I'm Remembered at All

My grandfather-in-law, David Mainse, will be remembered by many for generations to come. Grandpa was a tall man with broad shoulders and a voice like rolling thunder. I've spent my adult life speaking to people, and I know we shouldn't covet, but what I wouldn't give for a voice like his. People wonder sometimes what God sounds like. My guess is a lot like Grandpa.

David and his wife, Norma Jean, founded Crossroads in 1962. If grit is one ingredient in greatness, the other is Norma Jean. To all who knew them, it was universally understood Grandma was the great woman behind, or more accurately *beside*, the great man. Many would say they were a match made in heaven. There is no doubt they were a match made *for* heaven. Their commitment to sharing the love of Jesus was unparalleled. It wasn't displayed only in their television ministry, it shined brightest in their marriage. Their love and commitment for one another set an example we can all aspire to follow.

Many people will remember Grandpa. Not because he built a ministry that touched millions of lives in Canada and around the world, but because he treated every person he ever met like they were God's masterpiece. I was with Grandpa on several occasions when he was recognized by our server at a restaurant. The way he engaged with each of them was incredible. It was like the whole world disappeared and it was just him and that individual for a few moments. To him, it didn't matter if you were an executive or the busboy.

Grandpa had many gifts. Vision for his ministry was one; his voice another. To me, though, his greatest gift might have been the dreams he had for individual people, and his ability to see the true worth of every person.

Grandpa and Grandma pioneered Christian television in Canada and hosted a popular daily television program called *100 Huntley Street*. Grandpa became a household name throughout Canada, much like Billy Graham in America, and achieved remarkable fame and success. We have photos of Grandma and Grandpa with Prince Charles and Princess Diana, and letters from Ronald Reagan and other heads of state. In his years on television, he conducted more than 14,000 interviews. The students who graduated from his school of broadcasting pioneered television ministries all over the world. Currently, their programs present the gospel every day to a potential audience of over three billion people.

Yet with all the influence and fame he achieved, Grandpa never used it for his benefit. He wasn't perfect. He could be demanding and challenging to work for at times. He possessed a work ethic that tended to wear others out as Crossroads churned out new television programming and inspired others to create their own. Grandpa would be the first to tell you that though he built something incredible, he was remarkably human. His ministry and personality touched an entire nation and anyone who truly knew David Mainse understood, first and foremost, he was all about Jesus. After that, he was all about everyone else.

At a gala the night of the 50th anniversary of Crossroads, the host asked Grandpa during an on-stage interview, "David, what do you most want to be remembered for?"

Grandpa leaned back in his chair and folded his arms across his chest. A look of what appeared to be a mixture of confusion and contempt washed over his face. Everyone quit moving, some with glasses half-raised for a drink. An uneasiness settled in as Grandpa's countenance gave the impression he was annoyed by the question, even angered by it. His brow furrowed deeper, his eyes searched the ceiling until, finally, Grandpa cleared his throat, lowered his gaze to meet his host's, and in the full temper of his booming voice, he said something I'll never forget: "*I don't care if I'm remembered at all.*"

That sentence is one of the reasons you hold this book in your hands. Only time will tell the full ripple effect of Grandpa's answer. Its impact on my life alone has been profound. Seated toward the back of the room that night, his answer jarred me. I was trying to build a ministry at the time. Deep down, I wanted the level of success and influence he had achieved. To me, the host's question about his legacy was perfectly normal, but Grandpa was peeved by it. *Why?*

Because he genuinely did not view his influence, his platform, or his notoriety as something to be leveraged for his own gain. To Grandpa, it was all a gift from God. One that could only be used the way Jesus would, for the benefit of everyone but himself.

Not everyone wants to be famous, but we all want to have a legacy. Even if only for our children and friends. One of the many lessons I learned from Grandpa is that the best way to achieve a lasting impact is to quit caring about it and instead, focus on caring about everyone around you. Our lives and leadership can create a ripple effect that long outlasts our earthly lives. Not by focusing on ourselves, but by using our influence to uncover the potential of everyone else. In the end, our legacy is not what we achieve, but what others accomplish because of us.

Give Rather Than Get

Comedian Michael Jr. started his career asking the question, "How can I get laughs?" It sounds like an appropriate question for someone with his career. It worked well. The laughs rolled in during performances, until one night in Los Angeles just before he went onstage to perform, God gave him a change in mindset. Rather than asking how he could get laughs from the audience, he asked himself how he could give them opportunities to laugh.

Give, rather than get.

This subtle shift reaped benefits on and off the stage. On that night his performance was relaxed in a way he had never experienced before. It was a newfound freedom. He was simply there to offer a gift, not asking anything in return. With every chance he gave that night, the audience howled.

Michael Jr. had performed at that L.A. club many times before. After each show he spent time outside interacting with the crowd, taking pictures, and signing autographs, but that night he saw something he had never seen before. Across the street from the club was a homeless person. Michael Jr. doesn't believe that was the first time a homeless person had been outside the club after one of his performances. He believes the self-centeredness of the question driving his career had blinded him from seeing the person before and robbed him of the opportunity to help.

Following that experience, Michael Jr. founded *Funny for the Forgotten*, a non-profit that exists to make laughter commonplace in uncommon places. He regularly performs on skid-row and in prisons where he gives opportunities to laugh to those who rarely have them.[2]

That night, Michael Jr. learned a life-changing lesson. It's related to the one I learned from Grandpa the night of the 50th anniversary: living for what we can give is a far more enjoyable and rewarding than living for what we can gain.

Very Important Persons

Not long after I graduated college, a severe ice storm crippled Springfield, Missouri, where I was living at the time. We moved from house to house as different sections of the city lost power. Some areas went without electricity for over a week. I was scheduled to speak at an event, and I was determined to get there despite the blackout. It was, after all, in Orlando where the average temperature was sixty degrees higher than my current location. It took over seven hours to make the three-hour drive to the Kansas City Airport, where my direct flight to sunny Florida was waiting.

I took a cab to the hotel when I arrived, and that's when the confusion began. I realized I had no idea who booked my room at this hotel, and we couldn't figure out whose name the room was under. We tried my name, the name of the church I was speaking at, the pastor's name, the youth pastor's, too. Nothing worked and my calls to the event's organizers went unanswered.

We all have bad days. The young lady trying to check me in was having one, and it felt like I was the source. That she was growing more frustrated by the second would have been obvious to anyone anywhere near the lobby. I thought about leaving but remembered I had nowhere to go.

She excused herself and stepped into a back office to speak to the manager. I wasn't sure how this was going to go. After a tense few minutes, she returned but was a new person. The scowl that had been camping out on her face was gone. Smiling and upbeat she said, "I'm sorry sir, I see now you're a VIP guest at the hotel. Your suite is ready for you."

My *suite*? I was a *very important person*? My mom had always told me that, but how did the people at this hotel know? I fought to keep the surprise from showing on my face. I had no idea what she was talking about. Just then, the manager stepped out of the back room and introduced herself. It turns out she attended the church I was scheduled to speak at and had been the person who entered me into the system as a VIP. I had so much fun texting pictures of my huge suite to my friends back in Springfield. I couldn't wait for the power to come back on so they could recharge their dead phones and see them.

It's a shame, but we all treat people differently based on the information we have about them, just like the young lady trying to check me in at the hotel. Had the merchant community on St. Croix done this with young Alexander Hamilton, our nation wouldn't be what it is today.

We don't have to determine who is a VIP and who isn't. That's not our calling or the reason God has given us influence. We can treat everyone God brings into our lives like they have the potential to be the next leading lady or founding father. Who knows, they just might be.

There are wonders waiting in each of us. That includes *you*. This book is all about helping people discover their potential, but I'm not asking you to give up fulfilling your own. I'm arguing that the best way to discover yours is to make your life all about helping others realize theirs. I'm asking you to trust in the biblical principle of sowing and reaping. If you make your life about helping everyone else discover who they are, God will show you who you are.

Grandpa never could have imagined in 1962 that he would meet royalty as a result of his ministry or impact millions of people, but he didn't arrive there by fighting for his own success or worrying about his legacy. He did it by making his life all about Jesus and then about others.

Let's dispense with an excuse right now: you don't have to be the leader of a large ministry, a successful comedian, or someone with a particular pedigree in order to be someone's biggest fan. Whether you have influence in someone's life as their friend or boss doesn't matter. What matters is that when we see the potential in others, we do something about it.

How can we give our lives in service of others and their God-given potential? It requires a new mindset cultivated by asking the right questions. Instead of, "What can I gain?" it must become, "What can I give?" Rather than wondering, "How can I solidify my legacy?" we have to ask, "How can I help build yours?" Like Michael Jr., it will open our eyes to the potential of people around us who may have, up until now, been overlooked.

There is untold beauty in the lives of people all around us. Often, it's buried within the unnoticed and underappreciated people at our jobs, in our neighborhoods, and our churches. God is asking us to lift them up, call them over from the margins, and propel them to new opportunities that will create a ripple effect long after we're gone.

3

Vision for People

AT THE 1936 OLYMPIC GAMES in Berlin, the Germans won consistently. They also cheated, a lot. One of the most brazen offenses took place in the final race of the men's rowing competition. The stakes were incredibly high. Germany had won gold throughout the rowing competition and Hitler demanded victory in the closing and most prestigious event in the sport.

The fastest time trial for the gold-medal race belonged to the US team. They should have been assigned to lane one, which hugged the shoreline and was protected from the force of the wind. Instead, it was awarded to Germany. The US team was placed in lane six, far out into the waters and fully exposed to the fierce gale that whipped across the river.

Being exiled to lane six wasn't the US team's only setback. Don Hume, the rower who set the stroke for his teammates, was also gravely ill. During the race, he slipped into a semi-conscious state for a brief but tense moment. I can empathize; I experienced the same lack of consciousness frequently in my high school science class. No surprise here, but I was more of a history guy. The US team had more than their share of adversity, but one all-important thing remained in their favor: Bobby Moch, the boat's coxswain, refused to let them quit.[1]

The boats used for this class of rowing competition held nine people. The eight rowers had their backs to the finish line. They couldn't see where they were going and didn't know exactly when they'd arrive. The ninth team member, the coxswain (pronounced *cox-in*), was seated in the back of the boat. He faced the team and was the only one who could see the finish line. He steered the boat, increased the tempo of the strokes, and pushed his teammates to the breaking point if necessary.

In the closing meters of the final race, Moch propelled his team to achieve the unthinkable, calling for twenty "big ones," which are massive strokes requiring the utmost of rowers. They are usually reserved for dire situations or the final stretch. They leave rowers in agonizing pain, their bodies and muscles stretched to their limits. Behind for the whole race, Moch called for those twenty strokes as the gap was closing. The boys were in a dead heat with the Germans and the Italians.

The US team was pulling nearly forty strokes per minute. An incredible rate. Moch needed even more, but as they neared the finish, they were rowing beside the massive grandstand filled with thousands of German fans. Positioned in lane six, they were mere feet from the crowd. Waves of "Duetsch-land" from the roaring crowd thundered down on them, drowning out Moch's voice as he screamed for his team to up the stroke. Even Don Hume, now fully awake, and less than two feet from Bobby's face couldn't make out what he was shouting.

With no way to be heard, only yards from the finish line, neck and neck with the Germans and Italians, Moch began to smack the side of the boat hoping that they could at least feel the vibrations in the hull and know what it meant—*reach for the impossible.*

Miraculously, Moch's coded message was understood. With their hearts pounding, their bodies strained and exhausted, the boys ratcheted up the stroke to a new height. Through agonizing pain and with their chests on fire, they swung their oars, plunged them into the waters, and pulled with all their might in perfect unison. With one last magnificent stroke the boat surged across the finish line.[2]

We all deserve to have a Bobby Moch in our lives. Someone who has vision to see what we are truly capable of and calls us to achieve the impossible. Whether that person is a friend, parent, coach, or co-worker doesn't matter. We all need fans in our corner who will champion us and cheer us on. Moch was the smallest person in the boat and the only one without a paddle. It would have been all too easy to underestimate his value to the team, but he was essential to their victory. His voice, and his willingness to lift it above the noise, catapulted his team to greatness.

Vision for People

My friend Andy Estrella is one of those people who loves to

celebrate others. When I showed up at a restaurant to grab lunch with him, I didn't know I'd be getting a lesson about life and leadership, but I did know it would be a good time. Andy is one of those friends who makes a bad mood impossible. It's not just that he's hilarious. It's that Andy's love for people and his ability to see the best in them is unparalleled. It's also infectious. He encourages me to believe the best about others. I love being around him. It's like medicine for my weary soul.

That day, the conversation turned to leadership. Another friend who was with us began to pick Andy's mind about how he grows his team. Andy is a master at developing people. Turning those who are doers who get tasks done into developers who help others grow isn't easy. It requires a particular skill set. He was born with it. If Andy is breathing, someone else is being developed.

While sharing a platter of wings and waiting for our burgers to arrive, Andy finally put to words how he champions people and develops them into better people and leaders. Andy told us that it's not just about having great vision for your ministry or organization, although that is vital. It's about having what he calls *vision for people*. That's the real secret.

Vision for people is what coxswains have that allows them to push their teams to greatness. They can see in those in front of them what they often cannot see in themselves. Having vision for people is what all leaders need to succeed in helping others discover the true wonder God has lovingly fashioned within them.

The US team had never finished a race like the one for Olympic gold. Out in lane six, with the wind whipping against them, they powered their way through the final strokes with a grit no one can teach. It can't be bought or borrowed either. It's formed in environments where people believe in each other without reservation. Behind for the entire race, those strokes closed the gap in the final seconds and pushed the nose of the boat across the finish line.

In first place.

They had won by less than one second, but no one in the boat knew it yet.

Their momentum carried them from the crowd as they gasped for breath. What they had endured should not have been possible. They didn't know they were champions yet, but because of Bobby Moch, they had discovered that they could row as a team in absolute perfection.[3]

Bobby was the only one in the boat who could see the finish line that day, but it wasn't his primary focus. Bobby's eyes weren't solely on the finish line. His mind wasn't on the celebration that awaited them if they won. His focus was his team. He knew where the finish line was, all leaders must, but his vision was on his brothers in the boat. Helping them achieve their true potential was his first goal. The finish line, oddly enough, was second place for Moch.

What I'm learning from leaders like Andy and Bobby is that the best way to champion people we love and lead is to develop vision for them. It will not only help them realize their God-given potential, it will help them, and our teams, achieve the impossible.

Whether we're leading an organization attempting to hit a quarterly growth goal, coaching a team toward a championship, or just parenting our children to become responsible adults, we've all got a finish line we're trying to cross. Those goals aren't unimportant. Our dreams and the vision we have for achieving them can be a life-changing gift to others. But only if we develop vision for them *as people.*

The Investment

After five-and-a-half years of living in Oklahoma City, my wife, Andrea, and I moved to a suburb of Indianapolis, IN, to start Parkside Church. The day before we set out, Andrea had completed her journey toward earning her doctorate. Before a board of her mentors, she defended her dissertation titled, *HLA Class I Epitopes for Immunotherapeutic Targeting of Ovarian Cancer.* It's okay, I don't know what that means either. I think it means I married a genius. Because her brilliance matches her beauty, she passed with flying colors and was awarded a PhD in Immuno-Oncology.

When Andrea arrived back at our apartment, she discovered it had been completely packed into boxes for our move to Indiana. The night she was awarded a PhD she slept on an air mattress. I had already packed our bed into the moving truck. In hindsight, it wasn't the best way to celebrate her accomplishment. I'm not sure whether this incident, or the time I brought home a German Shepherd puppy without telling her, is worse.

The following morning, we began the two-day trek to Fishers, Indiana, to start a new life in a city we had never lived in before.

Over the next few months, we had a small group of people move there to help us plant the church. I'm still amazed by their courage to follow us on this new adventure.

As we began the process of starting the church, I quickly realized we would need a lot of support. I had plenty of questions and not too many answers. I was also becoming fast friends with ambiguity. If you've ever started your own business or set out on an adventure in life you were passionate about, then you know what these kinds of moments are like. They are a cocktail of excitement and anxiety. Part of the stress for me was the finances. It can cost a significant amount of money to start a church.

When the opportunity arose to have lunch with a fellow pastor who might invest in our church, Scott Wilson, I was excited to share my dream. We were still snacking on the chips and salsa when Scott told me he loved what we were doing. We had been together for about eleven minutes. Seriously, we hadn't even ordered our food yet. I had barely gotten through sharing our plans for launching a church in the Indianapolis area when Scott said he wanted to support us financially, to the tune of thirty thousand dollars. I would have danced to that tune if I wasn't so self-conscious about my lack of rhythm. Scott also told me about an upcoming retreat for church planters he was hosting. He wanted to pay for Andrea and I to join several other church planting couples. He wanted to invest in us. I was stunned.

In a matter of minutes, Scott decided he believed in what we were doing, but more than that, I realized he believed in me. For a guy who can be pretty insecure at times, that was reassuring. I wasn't sure how much I believed in myself at that point.

I had never done anything like this. I had never started a church, let alone built a team, developed a vision, raised funds, and created the necessary structures for a church to function *from scratch*. All I had ever done was speak at churches and events. I knew how to talk pretty well, that's it.

To this day, I don't know why, but Scott Wilson had vision for me. The confidence he had in me was contagious, and I was the one catching it.

The Shift

What I didn't know at the time was Scott had been leading people this way for about a quarter of a century. Turns out, he had a mindset shift while working at his first position in ministry as a youth pastor. Early on, Scott developed an unhealthy obsession with growing that ministry. His ego was in the driver's seat, and he was about to realize how that was keeping him from accomplishing what mattered most. Scott's desire for growth caused him to view his current students only as a means to an end. To him, they weren't individuals whose potential needed to be stewarded, they were collectively a tool he could leverage to increase attendance at his youth services. In the church world, attendance numbers can be toted around like trophies to impress our peers. Deep down we all know it's unhealthy, but it's a hard habit to kick. As Scott tells the story, it wasn't long before he had a striking moment of clarity.

Scott realized he had the job all wrong. The goal wasn't to *use* students to increase the size of his ministry. Those teenagers *were the job*. Having a growing ministry was the dream he was chasing. It was the finish line for his race. But unlike Bobby Moch, the finish line was his first priority, rather than his team. The people helping Scott run his race, in this case the teenagers attending his youth ministry, had become a commodity for him to use to achieve his dream. Because of the change in his approach, those students would become the dream. Scott was learning to have vision for people, not just for his ministry.

It's not that leaders like Scott and Andy don't know where the finish line is; they do. What they've discovered is a better way to get there.

Leaders who treat those around them like a means to an end reach their destination saying, "I did it." They only have vision for themselves. Those who focus on their team as their first priority still achieve their dreams. But they arrive saying, "We did it." Better still, the ones who are truly secure in who they are just say, "You did it." That's how leaders with vision for people sound.

Early in his career, Scott had a dream for his student ministry but he didn't have vision for each student as an individual made by God. He wasn't stewarding their potential. He was using it. They existed to help him accomplish his goal of a growing ministry.

That's not vision for people, that's an agenda.

Having agendas for others can turn them into pawns in a game they don't want to play. It's not a way we should ever live or lead. After his transformation, Scott realized he existed for his students, not the other way around. Their growth became his passion.

It's important to note, Scott never stopped striving to create a thriving youth ministry. He still wanted it to grow. There's nothing wrong with that dream. You don't have to give up on the dreams and goals God has given you either. The finish line for your marriage, your team, or organization doesn't have to change, but we do have to make a shift if we want to help those we love and lead discover their true potential. If we don't, we run the risk of burning out the very people we are called to build up. Never forget where the finish line is that God is calling you to cross, but make the people who are on the journey with you, sacrificing and serving to help you get there, your first priority. If we truly long to help those we love and lead discover who God has designed them to be, we must discard our agendas and become leaders who possess vision for people.

Champions

Bobby Moch and his friends in the boat deeply wanted to win. No doubt about it. They fought to get in that boat against talented competitors at the University of Washington. They endured a brutal training regimen to defeat the powerhouse schools of their day, like the University of Southern California and Princeton, in the qualifying races for the Olympics. They were enormously proud of what they had accomplished. They could taste victory when they arrived in Berlin.

But to win the gold on race day, Moch had to have vision for his teammates. As the coxswain, he was the only one in the boat without an oar. The only way he could contribute was with his voice, giving timely instruction and constant encouragement. If he didn't use his voice, he was dead weight. The boat didn't need a ninth rower.

It needed a voice with vision.

Because Moch championed his team to perfection, they won a victory for the ages. Winning a championship is meaningful; go for it. There's no reason to give up on that goal. But the greatest reward in life isn't crossing the finish line first or being ahead in the score when time expires. It's championing your teammates so they can discover the hidden greatness God has woven into them.

The boys in Moch's boat finished the race with their chests on fire and their muscles screaming in pain. They dropped their oars and collapsed on one another in utter exhaustion, but their hearts were full. Because even though they were spent, they hadn't been used. They weren't eight people who existed so Bobby Moch could win a gold medal. They were the eight people Moch championed, heart and soul. Because of his voice, and his vision for them as a team, they all became champions together.

I'm not always the fastest learner, I was born with a bit of a stubborn streak, but little by little I'm learning a meaningful lesson from leaders like Bobby, Scott, and Andy:

The word champion is a better verb than a noun.

If you're building a team of people to help you across your finish line, have vision for them as people, not pawns. There is untold potential in those God has surrounded us with both at home and at work. Be a voice full of vision for them. Call them to greatness. Champion them, heart and soul. There is no end to what you might achieve together.

There are victories ahead for you and the people alongside you. Always know where the finish line is, just don't wait until you cross it to celebrate them.

PART II

The Obstacles in our Path

"In the middle of every difficulty lies opportunity."[1]

Albert Einstein

4

10,000 Episodes

AFTER THIRTY YEARS OF DAILY programming, Grandpa's flagship television show, *100 Huntley Street*, reached a milestone few shows live to see; its 10,000th episode. That's more than double the number in the twenty-five-year run of *The Oprah Winfrey Show*. The hit sitcom *Friends*, which seemed to be on the air for ages, ended after ten seasons with a total of 236. To celebrate *Huntley Street's* achievement, family and friends from all over, as well as several of Grandpa's previous co-hosts, returned for the celebration.

During the special hour-long broadcast, Grandpa interviewed people who had hosted with him and a clear theme emerged in their stories. All of them kept thanking Grandpa for where they went after they finished working with him on *Huntley Street*. While each of them was working at Crossroads, God had given them dreams to do something else. And the person who had championed those dreams was the guy they were working for.

Sitting in the live studio audience that day, that jarred me. For perspective, over the years I have received numerous calls from friends who have been fired by their bosses for having a dream to do something else other than their current job. Frequently, they were fired *on the spot*. Like, the minute they expressed their God-given dreams to their boss they ceased to be employed. I heard a fellow pastor explain why this happens one time. It's because when we lead from insecurity it makes it difficult for anyone to win.[1] Insecurity can rob those we love of the leadership they desperately need. There is potential in them that will remain hidden if we cannot overcome this obstacle.

I had never experienced anything like what I was witnessing in the 10,000th episode. I now know it was a rare glimpse behind the scenes of a man who was incredibly secure. Being the champion of the dreams God gave other people, which meant they would be leaving Grandpa's ministry and going elsewhere, wasn't a fluke. It was a tradition. He had been doing it consistently for decades.

There is an incredible freedom that comes from being secure in who we are. It allows us to believe in others and what they can achieve, even if they go on to accomplish things far greater than we ever will. Security opens the door to a life that celebrates others. That has a vision for the dreams God has for those we lead and an unwavering conviction to support them.

Insecurity is a prison. A solitary confinement to a life inwardly focused. It's a pretty dark place. I've spent more than a few days there. Insecurity causes us to be confined to celebrating ourselves and touting our own achievements. It's ugly. I've lived this way too.

Thanks to heroes like Grandpa, I'm learning there is a better path for life and leadership. It's not for a select few. It's just for those who are brave enough to admit that it's not currently the one they're on and have the courage to change.

B-Level Speakers

I spent the first fourteen years of my career traveling for speaking engagements, mostly at church-related gigs. The evening time slot is prime time in the speaking world, reserved for the best and most well-known communicators. Lesser known and up-and-coming talent are often scheduled in the morning. Being assigned the first slot of the day was the kind of thing that could kick my insecurities into high gear.

Early in my career, I was invited to speak at the national youth camp for a group of associated churches across the Republic of Ireland and Northern Ireland. For many years, churches working with one another from both parts of the island would have been unthinkable. It was a fantastic privilege to be a part of it. I couldn't believe I had gotten the opportunity. But when they told me I would be the morning speaker each day for the week-long camp, my heart sank. *The morning speaker?* My head instantly filled with toxic thoughts about not being good enough. To me, it was like they were telling me I was less talented than the other communicators. I felt like a nobody. It wasn't true, but I was convinced of it at the time.

When I arrived at the camp as the "morning speaker" I felt that everyone was looking at me as the second-tier talent. So, I thought I had to find a way to convince everyone I wasn't a speaker of b-level abilities.

The week before I arrived in Ireland, I had been the evening speaker at a camp in Texas, the one who got his picture on all the promotional materials. That camp was one of the largest in all of the US with over one thousand students in attendance. Speaking at that camp made me feel good. It made me feel successful. Going to the next camp as the morning speaker ate at me. It feels so lame to say it now, but I kept trying to find ways to tell people I had been the evening speaker at the Texas camp. *Did I mention it was the largest camp in the country?* That's how each conversation went. It was brutal.

Worse yet, I was aware of what I was doing. I walked around the camp trying to creatively work the Texas camp into conversations with people I was just meeting for the first time. I wanted them to believe that I was somebody, that I was more talented than the morning time slot made me feel. It was ugly. At the time, I felt like I couldn't stop myself. No one likes self-promoters, and I soon found out that the Irish are uniquely gifted at humbling those who attempt to exalt themselves. Apparently, God gave most Irish people the same spiritual gift—*sarcasm.* They use it well.

Speaking at that same camp in Ireland a few years before I did, a friend of mine, we'll call him Brian because that's his name and he's guilty, told the audience he played college football at Oklahoma University. That was no problem, but then he tilted his chin upward and in a moment of self-assuredness, said, "*I could have gone pro.*" He moved right along in his message and forgot he had said it. At the end of the week, all the students divided into teams and had to write and perform a skit in front of the rest of the camp. I'll let you guess which phrase every single team included. Years later, that statement is still thrown around in a roast to Brian's temporary hubris.

I spent that week trying to prove to everyone I was a pro, but mercifully I was spared this treatment, although, I'll never know how or why. It's a miracle there isn't a whole generation of Irish people working the sentence, *"Did I mention it was the largest camp in the US?"* into their conversations to roast me.

Sometimes insecurity causes us to fall into the trap of feeling like it's our job to point out what makes us valuable or important. I tumbled into it headlong. It causes a form of memory loss that stops us from recalling why we all matter in the first place—we are God's masterpiece. There are wonders waiting in every one of us.

That week of camp, I missed golden opportunities to treat people like VIPs because I was too busy trying to convince myself and everyone else that I was one. The key to knowing our value isn't telling everyone else that we matter; it's agreeing with what God says about us. We are each his handmade work of art. We don't need to vocalize that truth. We need to internalize it. That's where the miracle happens.

When it does, we'll be well on our way to championing the potential in others. Even if it means they leave the nest at home, our team, or our staff at the office to pursue their dreams.

True Freedom

It was during the 10,000th episode of *100 Huntley Street* that God began to show me the incredible freedom security brings to a leader. When I was trotting around the camp in Ireland, feeling insecure about my talent, I needed a gift from everyone there. I needed them to validate me and convince me I was good enough. Listening to people who co-hosted with Grandpa over the years, I realized that when we are secure in who we are, our leadership doesn't *need a gift* from those who follow us. Our leadership *becomes a gift* to those who follow us. Being insecure robs us of our influence and leaves the potential in others undiscovered. We must emerge from the confinement of insecurity so we can focus on championing those around us.

The first time I sent chapters of my book to an editor, I forgot one thing—to run the spelling and grammar check first. After writing the second chapter and then adding a new ending to the first, I totally ran out of time, and in a rush to get home, feed my kids, and get out the door to soccer practice, I forgot to fix the errors before hitting send.

I was mortified. What kind of writer sends something to an editor without at least doing the basic Microsoft Word fixes? *The bad kind*, I thought. I figured it would be the only draft I ever sent and that my writing career would end before it began. I've learned now that it wasn't a big deal at all. But at the time, it felt like it was.

There are some chapters in our lives that have received more editing than others. Some have had the basic spelling and grammar check. Others have been re-written so much they bear no resemblance to the original. That's what God does. But there are some chapters we're more hesitant for him to read. The problem is when we keep God out, those chapters don't stay hidden from God or those closest to us. We're just unaware of how painfully obvious they are to everyone else.

For me, my insecurity is one chapter I have been slow to submit to God. I bet you've got some chapters like that too. Who wants to admit they are insecure? I've spent most of my life trying to fool everyone, myself included, that it wasn't a problem. For a long time, I failed to realize everyone else could see it far better than I could anyway. Little by little, with a lot of God's help and consistent input from great people around me, I'm gaining more freedom from insecurity. The most beautiful part is I'm not the only beneficiary—everyone I love and lead is too.

The White City

In 1893, the White City was built in Chicago to celebrate the 400th anniversary of Columbus' voyage to America. It was an exhibition of colossal proportions, covering 690 acres with 200 newly constructed buildings and cultural displays from 46 countries worldwide. Throughout its six-month run, 27 million people attended—a number equal to nearly half the US population at the time.[2]

Electric light was in its infancy, and the city was designed to dazzle the world at night lit up by tens of thousands of new bulbs designed by Westinghouse Electric. The white buildings bathed in the yellow glow of incandescent light was a sight to behold. It was inspiring, but it was also an illusion. The city's structures were made to look like gleaming white stone, but they were really just sticks and plaster. The whole thing could have been brought down by one carelessly discarded cigarette butt and a gentle breeze. None of those buildings survive today. They were never meant to.

We do this in our own lives. We build a façade to present something we think others want to see. I've tried it countless times by projecting an image of greater achievement, success, or security. I've attempted to project an image of myself that would impress others, but it was actually an illusion.

I struggled with this a lot in the beginning of my ministry. When you start out in your career as a traveling evangelist there is an easy way to create an aura of importance.

Travel internationally.

It's a handy tool you can use if you're building a façade. You get to describe yourself using phrases like "international evangelist" and call your ministry "world-wide." People equate traveling far with being important. It's a way for people in my field to make things feel larger than they are.

Within the first year of my ministry, I had the chance to travel to Eastern Europe. We flew into Austria, but spent most of our time in Bratislava, the capital city of Slovakia. It was an amazing ten-day trip and was the first time I spoke to an audience who didn't share my native language. Using an interpreter and learning to connect with people whose culture differed from mine was an enlightening experience.

Before I even deboarded the plane in the US my insecurities were already tempting me to describe my ministry in grander terms. That temptation was heightened by the fact that a college friend who graduated with me from Central Bible College had also become an evangelist. We never wanted the comparison, but all of our friends seemed to measure our ministries against each other. Now, I had the chance to make my ministry sound bigger than his by styling myself a globe-trotting evangelist.

My insecurities were causing me to look for my value in the wrong places. It made me think and do a lot of silly things, but the desires were real. And I gave into the temptation. I was now an *International Evangelist with a World-Wide Ministry.* I was only a year into my career, but already I had some notches in my belt, or so I thought.

It's laughable now, but my insecurities and lack of self-worth were causing me to become something I never wanted to be—a smarmy seeker of self-importance.

I'm not sure what the dictionary definition of smarmy is, but I think it's someone who makes everything they do sound bigger than it really is because they don't understand how much they already matter to God.

We can all be experts at showing others what we want them to see, but we're mostly fooling ourselves. People did it in Jesus' day too. In one memorable example, a rich man tried to act like he had it all together in a conversation with Jesus. Jesus saw straight through the sticks and plaster and told the man to sell everything and give it to the poor. It wasn't that Jesus just wanted the rich man to *do something*; he wanted him to *become someone*—his true self, not the illusion created by his wealth.

Once we stop living an illusion, Jesus can transform us into the ideal. It will be a process, not a moment. Grandpa didn't arrive there quickly either, but we can become secure and as we do, we will become more open handed with those we love. We'll be the champion the people around us are desperate for and help them discover the wonders waiting within them.

The Son of Man

There is only one time in the Bible where Jesus talked directly about leadership. It's in a fascinating and rich story in the tenth chapter of Mark's account of Jesus' life. After explaining how those with influence and authority misuse it, Jesus told his followers that they had to do precisely the opposite. They had to use their leadership for the benefit of everyone but themselves.

The final verse in the story is one of the most quoted statements Jesus made. He said that he didn't come into this world to be served by others, but instead to serve everyone, ultimately by giving his own life to save us. It's a beautiful verse, but there is a part of it that often goes unnoticed. The verse is a proclamation of what Jesus plans to do and how he plans to do it, but that isn't how it starts. It begins with a statement of identity.[3]

Jesus opens by referring to himself as the "Son of Man." It's an intentionally cryptic title. No one fully understood what Jesus meant by it, and even his closest followers wouldn't comprehend it until after his resurrection.

The title "Son of Man" comes from one of those chapters in the Old Testament we often skip over. It's an apocalyptic dream full of creatures that sound like they should be guarding a cave of unimaginable treasures in a novel by Tolkien. Essentially, Daniel chapter seven is a story of a person who, after an intense season of suffering, is carried on the clouds to heaven and seated at the right hand of God Almighty. This person, called the "Son of Man", is enthroned in heaven in a place equal to God.

Jesus told his followers he came to serve them and to give his life for their sake freely. How could he live that way? Because he knew who he was. For Jesus, there were no sticks and plaster. No fake version of himself to project. Jesus knew his true identity, and he didn't have to *tell* everyone because he lived his whole life to *show* us clearly that he was the person described in Daniel's vision—he was the one who would suffer to save us and be rewarded by his Father in heaven.

Jesus is the most remarkable example of a leader who was fully secure in who he was. He was so rooted in his mission and identity that his life was given as a gift to his followers. His example of secure leadership isn't repeated often enough by his followers, but with his help, we can do it. Grandpa wasn't perfect, but he consistently championed his staff and made sacrifices for their dreams to be realized.

The 10,000th episode was a celebration not only of the dreams

Grandpa had for *Crossroads* and *100 Huntley Street*, but a towering testament to the beauty of the brand of leadership exemplified in Jesus. Grandpa had a corporate dream he was asking people to join, and it often cost a lot to follow his high-octane leadership. Because he had banished insecurity, he gained remarkable influence in people's lives and was able to use it for their benefit. Rather than burning people who developed a dream different from his, he championed them.

Recently, someone asked me what I am running away from and what I am running towards. After a short reflection, I said I am running away from not being good enough and toward being secure in who I am. I'm not sure what lap I'm on, but I know it's the right race. It's the right one for you too. It doesn't matter what lap you're on either. Like Forrest Gump, just keep running and running as you get closer to the goal.

There are people following you who are counting on you to stay in that race. Your life and leadership are the gifts they need. Whether it's your friends, spouse, kids, a division of a company, or an entire corporation, those people are worth your effort to understand who God made you be and become secure in your true identity.

5

Give Credit Away

IN THE MID-NINETEENTH CENTURY THE Lamme family farm, located on the outskirts of Springfield, OH, was a hive of creativity. Young Benjamin Lamme loved to tinker with mechanics and concoct experiments to understand how things worked. He was particularly fascinated by things that rotated quickly. It's no surprise that after graduating with a degree in engineering from the University of Ohio, Lamme only farmed for a few short months before taking employment at *Westinghouse Electrical*, where he would quickly rise to become the chief engineer for the rest of his career.

Lamme jump-started his time at Westinghouse by inventing a more efficient design for an induction motor based on a previous patent. Westinghouse was impressed, and Lamme would become best known for designing the massive generators that harnessed the waters of Niagara Falls to generate electricity. By the time his dizzying career wound to a stop, Lamme had been awarded a whopping one hundred and sixty-two patents. His accomplishments and awards are only known to us, however, because he worked for a man like George Westinghouse. Had he found employment with Westinghouse's chief rival, Thomas Edison, Lamme's name might be lost both to us and to history.[1]

Taking Credit

Minds like Edison's never stop. They solve problems in their sleep. His brilliance as an inventor is well documented and deserved. His voice was the first to be recorded and played back for others to hear using a phonograph he designed, and he created a working light bulb that was long lasting and cheap to produce—a first for all the brilliant people involved in the race for this prized invention, but among his incredible giftings as an inventor, promoter, and businessman, sharing credit with others was not one of them.

To be fair to Edison, I wouldn't always finish first in a race to give credit to others either. My ego and insecurities have gotten in the way more than I would like to admit. My guess is yours have a time or two as well, but generously giving credit to others for their contributions and creativity is one of the most powerful ways to encourage those we are championing. Recognizing the contributions of others meets a need we all possess: to be seen and appreciated.

Renovations

We love our home. It was over forty years old when we bought it, and some of it hadn't been updated since it was built in the late seventies, like the pink accented wallpaper and pink countertops in the hall bathroom upstairs. We make the kids use it and keep the door closed when guests come over.

We completely renovated the den and an adjacent bedroom on the main level taking certain parts of it down to the studs. We laid new flooring throughout and installed a ceiling fan in the center because there was no lighting in the ceiling previously. Apparently, having no ceiling lights in rooms was once a trend. I guess people were really into lamps back then.

The renovated rooms are often noticed by our guests and there are a lot of comments and compliments about them. People typically ask who we had do the work and I find myself responding, "I did it." To be honest, it is a half-truth at best. My father and father-in-law both helped me throughout the process.

When people ask who did the work, why do I tell people I did it and allow them to interpret that as literally me doing it all by myself?

The psychology behind why I take credit for it isn't hard to figure out. The rooms are really nice and it feels good to be complimented. I want the credit because I want to feel good.

And therein lies our opportunity. Sharing credit with others for their contributions is one of the simplest and most powerful ways to build them up, because it feels as good to them as it does to all of us.

Hogging credit isn't a trait that will endear us to people or attract others to want to be around us for the long haul. It can hurt people who are attempting to help us, and potentially push away the very people we need most to accomplish our dreams.

Give it Away

The incredible work ethic and brilliant mind of Thomas Edison are legendary. He famously ended his wedding night working in his lab. It's also well known that a staggering one thousand ninety-three patents were awarded to him in his lifetime. Unsurprisingly, none of them were for romance. What is lesser known is that many of those patents were based on the inventions and work of the employees of Edison's lab. In his businesses, Edison did not allow patents to be filed under any name other than his own no matter who made the discovery.

In contrast, George Westinghouse, who employed Lamme and many others like him, would not allow any patents to be filed in his name for the inventions of others. Without this policy, Benjamin Lamme's one hundred and sixty-two patents would have been added to the three hundred sixty-one Westinghouse was awarded. The addition of just Lamme's patents is enough to equal almost half of Edison's total. No one has ever counted, but if all of the patents awarded to employees at George Westinghouse's companies during his working career were added together, and put in Westinghouse's name, the total would easily rival, if not surpass, that of Edison's.[2]

Which begs a question that will never be answered. Was Edison or Westinghouse the greater inventor?

It doesn't matter. And Edison won the battle forever already anyway. His name is synonymous with inventor the same way Einstein's is with genius.

The bottom line is: Edison was an egotistical and difficult man to work for and was cut-throat in his attempts to bring down his rival inventors and fellow businessmen. Westinghouse was a kind and generous man who wanted those who worked for him to get credit for their work and creativity. Edison was larger than life and could control a room just by entering it. Westinghouse, in contrast, didn't even like to be photographed.

When Benjamin Lamme, and many others like him, became employed by Westinghouse it forever determined whether or not he would receive credit for his work and contributions to the field of electrical engineering.

Westinghouse's employees loved working for him. Edison's often did not. It wasn't all a matter of different personalities. Some traits of personality may make giving credit to others easier, but it's possible for all of us. Edison could have been like Westinghouse in this way, but he had a goal that excluded giving others credit for their contributions.

Edison longed to be famous and to be labeled as the greatest inventor of all time.

This goal made Edison the father of the uniquely American idea of creating a personal brand and turning your own name into a marketable commodity. Edison splashed his name and face onto everything possible, marketing *himself*, and not just his products, in a way never done before. Athletes like Michael Jordan may have improved on the idea, but it was an Edison original. It has been adopted in our world today by people in all walks of life, from politicians to pastors.

You might say Edison's greatest invention was his own fame.

While it might seem alluring, this lust for recognition and notoriety always comes with a cost. Edison's out of control ego caused collateral damage, intended or not. Failing to credit others for their contributions will drive away the most gifted and brightest employees, volunteers, and friends, as they search to find a place where they can be valued and appreciated. In Edison's life, this led to the greatest loss his lab had ever experienced.

The Current War

The war to satisfy America's growing appetite for electricity was intense. Edison and Westinghouse were locked in battle. Edison's direct current, or DC, was being implemented across America but had major limitations. The electricity his DC power stations generated could only travel about a mile, requiring multiple stations to service even a small city. In an interesting twist of history, the man who would solve this problem, creating the alternating current we use today, worked in Thomas Edison's lab. His name was Nikola Tesla.[3]

His invention would be the key to winning the war to provide electricity to America. For a short time, Edison had it within his grasp.

In June of 1884, Tesla began working at *Edison Machine Works*, and the boss quickly noticed his potential. Edison asked him to work on making improvements to his DC motor, promising a substantial bonus if Tesla succeeded. We don't know what improvements Tesla designed because when he asked for the bonus six months later, Edison refused. Tesla quit soon after.

What we do know is that the concept for the brushless AC motor Tesla would later build came to him while out for a stroll two years before his brief stint with Edison. That AC motor would transform how electricity could be harnessed and distributed. Tesla's invention would later win the war for George Westinghouse.

Edison had the man who could have catapulted him to victory in the most profitable enterprise he ever attempted, but his ego would not allow him to work with someone who's abilities rivaled his own.

His inability to share credit with people like Tesla—and pay them the money they deserved—cost Edison not only a fortune in lost contracts, it ripped control of his flagship enterprise from his hands. The investors who pushed Edison out also removed his name from the company he founded, rebranding it *General Electric*. For the man who longed to make his name famous, it was one of the lowest points in his life.

The Most Creative Man

With his love for the spotlight, Grandpa's personality more closely mirrored Edison's. He cherished being center-stage and was the furthest thing from camera shy, but unlike Edison, Grandpa was a master at championing those he loved and led by giving them full credit for their accomplishments and contributions.

I noticed this habit quickly as I began to spend time with him when I was dating Andrea. One of the things that immediately stood out to me was his willingness to share credit with others when achieving his dreams. Grandpa had built a ministry that made him a household name in Canada. When he passed away, one of Canada's largest newspapers based in Toronto, *The Globe and Mail*, announced that "Canada's Pastor" was gone. He was an Edison in his field.

But when he talked of his successes, he always spoke of the people who had made it all happen. He made it clear that without the brilliant and hardworking people at Crossroads, his dreams never would have become a reality.

Some of Grandpa's favorite stories to tell were of the pavilions Crossroads built at several World Expos, visited by millions of people. These were massive projects, requiring around the clock efforts from a staggering number of workers. The quality of the award-winning pavilions, and the impact they made for Jesus, were among Grandpa's proudest achievements. It was rare to eat a meal with him without hearing a story related to one of the expos.

He would regularly highlight the brilliance of architect, Rob Adsett, who designed an award-winning pavilion for Expo 2000 in Hanover, Germany. The centerpiece of the exhibits housed in several of Crossroads' pavilions featured a musical score written by Bruce Stacey, titled *The Scroll*. Grandpa teared up every time he mentioned it. He was so moved by the power of Bruce's music, and the talent he possessed to write it. He repeatedly referred to Bruce as the most creative man he ever met.

It was in the culture of Crossroads, where credit was freely given to everyone by the man at the top, that the creativity of people like Stacey and Adsett, and scores of others, truly flourished. To Grandpa, his ministry only had the reach and impact it achieved *because* of these people. All of them would argue it was Grandpa's visionary leadership. Grandpa wouldn't dismiss that, but he would say that was only part of it, and that it would have accomplished nothing without the brilliance and God-given talent of those surrounding him.

They went further together than they ever could have apart, but what kept them on the same team was Grandpa's willingness to give credit to those who truly deserved it. Grandpa achieved his dreams, and the God-given potential of those around him was not only discovered, it was openly and beautifully celebrated.

Credit can be given away to others all around us in every circumstance. It doesn't matter if we're working hard around the house or on the job. Whether we're trying to champion our family or friends, a new hire or our longest tenured employee, our star player or a kid who sits the bench, noticing their abilities and their contributions is a universal way to help them see their true worth and the potential they possess.

Hogging credit is not only egotistical, it's sloppy stewardship of the God-given potential of those around us. If we truly want others to see the masterpiece God has created them to be, then celebrating their accomplishments by giving them credit is a skill we must master. Refusing to freely acknowledge the importance of the contributions others have made keeps the spotlight trained on us, the exact opposite of what we should want if we are attempting to be someone's biggest fan.

Sharing credit with others isn't only the most enjoyable way to build up those we love and lead, it's the best way to attract other brilliant and talented collaborators. If Edison had celebrated Tesla the way Westinghouse did for Lamme, or the way Grandpa did for Bruce and so many others, then he may not have lost his company or the war to provide America with electricity.

We can build our brand and craft our own legacy by hogging credit and putting all the patents in our own name, but not without paying the same price. It will cost us relationships with those who were meant to help us achieve our dreams and whose potential we could have discovered. Ego is a hard thing to exile, but it's worth it.

6

The Pain Scale

MY SON DECLAN AND I were out for a drive one afternoon when we passed the elementary school he would begin attending in a few months. Having a child start kindergarten is a strange moment for parents. It's one of the first times you realize how fast your kids are growing up.

As we passed the building, Declan said to me in his cute little voice, "I'm going to go there for a little while, and then I'm going to grow up and have kids."

I laughed, maybe a little too hard. I pointed out, gently, that he skipped a few stages of life. Like facial acne and marriage.

If we had the choice to skip seasons of our lives, we would likely choose the ones that caused us the most pain. It's understandable for sure. We would pass over the lies spoken about us, the broken relationships, the lost loved ones, and a whole host of other hardships that life can bring.

We all know we can't become exempt from experiencing difficult seasons in life, and even if we could, what would the cost be?

While toiling with writing my first book, I decided to attend a short retreat with a group of about thirty writers. In the opening session, the idea was to go around the room and introduce ourselves and share about our writing aspirations. We all should have known what was coming when the first person began to cry, sharing about her painful journey through divorce. She opened the floodgates.

Others shared about losing loved ones, going through a divorce of their own, and childhood trauma. What struck me is that we were *all* planning to write from our pain. We do it to reach for what we don't understand, and to make sense of what we experience. Humanity has done this for centuries.

Given a choice, many people in the room might have been tempted to detour around the very seasons of life that led to the books they planned to write.

As we drove past his school, Declan hopped from kindergarten to parenthood in one leap. He can't skip middle school any more than my fellow writers and I could take a pass on our seasons of pain. No one is exempt from difficult seasons in life, which leaves us with the question: *What do we do with our pain?*

If we're passionate about developing others, we must learn to process our hurts and heartaches in a healthy way. Unresolved pain narrows our field of view. Holding on to hurt and refusing to process it places blinders on us that blocks the vision we could have for those we love. People around us remain undeveloped, and we become increasingly focused on ourselves.

The Pain Scale

On a fateful spring afternoon, scores of tornadoes ripped through thirteen states in America's heartland. With hundreds dead and thousands injured, emergency workers struggled to provide care. Countless homes, businesses, and lives lay in tatters. It took mother nature only moments to accomplish unimaginable destruction and loss.

In the 1970s, tornadoes were terrifying not only for their destructive power, but also for their mystery. No one knew how they formed or how to predict them. Today we possess all that knowledge, primarily because of the relentless drive of one man, Tetsuya Theodore "Ted" Fujita. In the aftermath of the outbreak, like a detective scouring for clues, Fujita sifted through the rubble in an attempt to understand what had caused the deadly storms. He believed studying patterns in the damage held the key to the secrets of the outbreak.

Thirty-five years of Ted Fujita's brilliant life were dedicated to understanding tornadoes. His research has saved countless lives by increasing our ability to predict them. He created a scale for measuring the size of a tornado based on the damage left in its wake, naming it after himself, the *Fujita Tornado Scale*. The scale was from one to five with the most damaging tornadoes receiving a rating of Fujita 5 on the scale, or an F-5, as they are more commonly called.

In retirement, Fujita's health began to fail. Doctors were perplexed and unable to diagnose the pain in his feet and legs. With a kind of dedication only Fujita could muster, he studied, chronicled, and charted his pain with precision. Then he created a second scale, this time for his pain. The scale ranged from 1-10, measuring from mild discomfort while walking to unimaginable pain.[1]

We may not have created a scale for ours, but rating, compartmentalizing, or categorizing our pain can be our instinct. It's not one we should follow. The answer isn't to assign our pain a number, but to look it in the eye.

If we refuse to truly face our deepest hurts, our unresolved pain becomes an unreliable co-pilot in our journey to become who God made us to be and can rob us of the opportunity to help others discover their worth and fulfill their potential.

Pain-filled Poetry

The book of Psalms is one of the greatest collections of poetry in history. We don't know precisely how many inspired writers contributed, but the poems are full of pain and questions longing to be answered. If the writers had somehow been saved from experiencing low points in life, we wouldn't have their poetry. If David hadn't experienced want and been afraid for his life, we wouldn't have the most peace-filled poem in scripture, the twenty-third Psalm. We'd be poorer for it.

The Psalms are easy to love because they sound like us. The writers didn't know what to do with their pain either. Most of us, however, don't do what they did. I don't mean turning searing pain into soaring poetry. We don't get honest with God or others about our struggles.

When Andrea and I welcomed our third child into the world, our son Rowan, I realized there were some things I had forgotten since Declan was born more than four years earlier. For one, they sleep much as eighteen hours a day. If only it were eighteen *straight* hours. And, of course, they cry a lot. Every time they are in need, unhappy, or hungry, they loudly let you know. When babies are hurting, they *never* fail to cry.

I'm not sure when it happens, but there comes a point in life we stop sharing our pain and begin trying to cover it up. Crying out for help is our default setting, but hiding our pain is a learned habit. The longer I live the more I realize it doesn't serve us well.

As we strive to unveil the hidden potential of those around us, we will be called to the delicate task of helping them navigate their brokenness. First, we must learn to face our own. If we refuse, we run the risk of our mismanaged pain pulling us far off course and eventually arriving at the wrong destination entirely.

Circling Our Suffering

My journey of facing my pain has involved more laps than I intended. Perhaps yours has too. I have always deeply struggled with not being accepted. I took a personality test once and the results listed my greatest fear: social rejection. It could not have been more accurate.

In the early years of planting our church, my feelings of rejection peaked. I was feeling deeply unwanted and alone and was rapidly spiraling downward. It's often said that it's lonely at the top.

Working alone each day I was finding this to be especially true. Even more so because everyone else on my team was a decade younger and had far more in common with each other than with me. I felt like an outsider in the very thing I was creating.

Rather than talking with friends or taking it to God, I chose to push it aside. I was hoping my hurt would somehow dissipate and disappear over time.

On a trip with a member of my staff that I genuinely believe in, I had the opportunity to help him grow. Those uninterrupted days were a golden opportunity to learn more about him and call out the wonders within him, but my refusal to face my pain shifted my focus from his potential to my sorrows. It obscured my vision for him and robbed us both of an incredible chance to grow together, which was my greatest passion and the whole point of the excursion.

We were looking for something to do after lunch when we began to walk around an outdoor shopping area. As we began to talk, the intense strain from my unresolved pain caused me to snap. I began to vent about my perception of how he was treating me, the lack of respect I was being shown by our whole team, and my belief that none of them truly cared about me as a pastor or a person. None of it was true, but it was how I felt at the time.

It was horrible.

I was sickened by what I was saying, but I kept going. We circled the shopping center for almost *two hours.*

I was a leader who longed to discover the wonders God has woven into every person, but I was losing my way. Hiding how we've been hurt doesn't lead to healing. Instead, it allows it to simmer in our souls like a pressure cooker until one day it reaches a boiling point and we explode, causing more damage to ourselves and potentially everyone under our influence too.

I took the opposite path of the Psalmists whose honesty opened the door to God's helping hand. When we aren't honest about the hurt we carry through life, there is little chance for healing, moving on, or growing into who we are supposed to be. There's another risk too. We risk being able to focus on the people around us that we're trying to champion. If Pete Zamperini had been swallowed by pain, he wouldn't have been able to be Louie's biggest fan and drive him to become a champion. The co-hosts of Grandpa's show may not have gone on to accomplish their God-given dreams if Grandpa had been consumed by hurt because he wouldn't have been able to selflessly cheer them on.

Directionally Challenged

I have a friend named Jack who is directionally challenged. Even in the city where he has lived his whole life he still needs GPS to get to the grocery store. He's amazing in his own right but is a terrible co-pilot. If Jack is in charge of directions, you had better leave early and have a full tank of gas because you're headed for the "scenic route." On a trip from St. Louis to Indianapolis, Jack once wound up near Chicago before realizing he had taken a wrong turn.

If we don't deal with our pain it will become a co-pilot for our lives and our leadership, re-routing us to either avoid more hurt or avenge the past. If our destination is championing the people in front of us, pain will send us on inconvenient and costly detours. It's hard to lead, love, and celebrate others when our pain is sitting shotgun. We will be slow to affirm people who have hurt our feelings, we will try to get even with those who have abused our trust, and we will forfeit the hard-won influence with others that we have accumulated.

Hiding my hurt opened the door to being led by it. After my embarrassing two-hour rant, I slowly began to realize my pain had become an unreliable co-pilot for my journey, and I was becoming a leader who beats down the very people he is called to build up. On my journey to become the biggest fan of those I love and lead, I was rapidly becoming the exact opposite.

If we attempt to champion those around us, but refuse to face our unresolved pain, our vision for people will remain clouded. Refusing to work through our seasons of suffering is like studying the damage left behind by a tornado, but never removing the debris or beginning to rebuild. Resolving pain doesn't look like creating a scale to measure it like Fujita. It also doesn't look like hiding or ignoring it like I did.

Forsaken

WWJD bracelets took my middle school by storm. If you weren't alive back then or had your head buried in the sand during the 1990s, that stands for *What Would Jesus Do?* Wearing WWJD apparel was like a flag that all serious people of faith had to wave. In many situations, it's a helpful question to ask ourselves. However, there is a better one we can ask when it comes to handling pain: *What Did Jesus Do?*

Jesus didn't live a life void of pain. He was hated and despised by the powerful and mocked and humiliated by the self-righteous. Worse yet, his best friends betrayed him.

It's not hard to pinpoint Jesus' greatest moment of agony. It was so severe it would have stretched even Fujita's imagination and ability to categorize it. When Jesus carried his cross through a crowded street in Jerusalem, he wasn't just reeling from the scourging his back received at the hands of a Roman soldier, he was in deep emotional agony from being abandoned by his closest friends. In those fateful moments, Jesus was discovering what it felt like to be totally alone.

How do we know that? Because a few short hours later, suspended on the cross, Jesus cried out, *"My God, my God, why have you forsaken me?"* Those words weren't his; he borrowed them. When Jesus was in his greatest moment of anguish, he reached for the Psalms.

When my mother-in-law, Ann, received her cancer diagnosis, she spent hours reading and praying the Psalms. She said they gave her the freedom to be honest with God about her questions and anger. That is a beautiful freedom. It cost the Psalmists dearly to offer it to us. Too bad we often pass it by.

Jesus was leaning into that liberty when he quoted Psalm 22 from the cross—he was telling his Father exactly how he felt. We should try it too, even if it means saying things to God that our Sunday School teachers wouldn't approve. The path to healing isn't through Fujita's scale, or my attempts to hide it, it's through Jesus' example of honesty with God.

Whatever pain we don't resolve, we repeat. When this inevitably happens, as it did for me, it will cost us the ability to champion those we love and lead. Our influence will be squandered, and their God-given potential will remain hidden.

Hell Week

The third week of training for Navy SEALs is legendary. In five and a half days, the participants are allowed a total of four hours of sleep. For some of us, that's a Sunday afternoon nap. Trainees receive ample food, but they fall asleep on their plates from exhaustion. They pass out and plunge into the water paddling their boats and have to be rescued by teammates. Their bodies and minds are pushed to extreme limits, approaching hypothermia one moment and experiencing hallucinations the next. Debilitated by fatigue, they are asked to perform tasks and make decisions throughout. They named it Hell Week for good reason.[2]

When the one hundred thirty-two hours have passed, the most demanding training in the US military leaves soldiers with the knowledge that their teammates will never give up on them. Their shared experience of pain creates a bond that cannot be broken, even on the battlefield.

If they tossed a football on the beach instead of sitting next to each other for hours cradling a log the size of a telephone pole above their laps, the result would be different. They don't call it *Heaven Week.* You can't become teammates who will have each other's backs in life and death by playing games and eating barbeque.

Common Ground

My son couldn't go from kindergarten to having kids of his own in a single bound, and no matter how much we long to skip the painful seasons of life, we know it's not an option. Even if it were, we would be giving up something that provides one of the most effective tools we have for developing others: common ground. If the SEALs skipped Hell Week, they would never know the powerful bond of friendship experienced by those who share a common struggle, and they wouldn't trust one another in life and death situations. If my fellow writers at the retreat somehow passed over pain in their lives, they would have forfeited the books they wrote because of those experiences. If Jesus had skipped coming to earth and giving his life for us, he would have missed out on understanding our suffering and sorrows as a fellow human being.

I'm not glad any of us have been through hurt, but hardship affords us an opportunity to connect with others. We are able to help those around us best when we can relate to them. Jesus knew this well. Shared pain allows us to understand each other even if we didn't experience it together like the SEALs.

There is no need to hide our wounds from God like I did. In some of the darkest times of our lives God receives radio silence from us. That's a radical departure from Jesus' approach on the cross. We also don't need to measure our pain like Fujita did. Our path to healing begins by being honest with ourselves and with God about our suffering.

The road to healing is one we must travel if we want to unveil the wonders hidden within those around us. If pain becomes our co-pilot, we'll leave St. Louis headed for Indianapolis, but end up near Chicago instead. Unresolved pain will rob us of our influence, lead us to become inwardly focused, and leave those we believe in most undeveloped and underappreciated.

It's not an easy road. I love that Jesus didn't offer us an explanation, just an example. Jesus showed us we don't need to offer God a false representation of how we feel. We don't need to clean it up for God and make it G-rated. If we did, Jesus would recognize it anyway. If we're genuine, what we'll find is many of the seasons of life we might have passed over are the ones God will use to draw us closer than ever before, both to himself and to those we love and lead. That doesn't mean there aren't some we would skip over no matter what beauty might come from them, but it does mean there will be moments of pain God will use to shape us into the master-piece he created us to be.

7

Moonshot

SCATTERED ACROSS NASA'S FACILITIES IN Langley, Virginia, scores of mathematicians worked tirelessly to accomplish a dream that captivated the minds of Americans throughout the 1960s: landing a man on the moon. To eventually reach the lunar surface, they would first have to chart the necessary trajectory to lead an astronaut in orbit back to Earth. Precise calculations had to be made to safely return the spaceship and its pilot, but there was one significant problem. The math to formulate those equations did not exist.

Langley needed an expert in analytic geometry, but they didn't know where to find one. I can't blame them. I wouldn't know where to look either. I'm doing good most days to find my shoes and my car keys. NASA lacked a computer—which back then was a person, not a machine—who could do the math, crunch the complicated numbers, and calculate the correct trajectory for a safe return to earth.

NASA's goal of landing the first person on the moon was crystal clear. They knew exactly what they were trying to achieve. Starting our church, I had a well-defined dream too. To create a place where people could discover their God-given potential. I also had a similar problem to NASA's. I didn't know how to do the math. Leading those I love in a way that would truly unearth their potential wasn't something I knew how to do. I had clarity in where I wanted to go but not in how to get there.

I had a second problem, too. In my mind, I was convinced that I *did* know the math. Believing I was already leading people well and helping them discover their potential created a desperate need for course-correction, but my lack of self-awareness about my own leadership kept me from making any adjustments, leaving people around me stagnant in their development. Instead of championing people, I slipped into a familiar way of leading that I had seen and experienced before. One that led me in the opposite direction I desired. It would be a painful moment when I realized I was not the leader I longed to be. Fixing my lack of self-awareness would remedy my first problem, but in the early days of the journey I didn't know that either.

Lacking self-awareness is a costly mistake. Without an eye-opening realization, a deficit of awareness likely would have cost NASA first place in the race to land a man on the moon. Being unaware slows our own growth because we think we're farther along in the journey than we really are, stifles our ability to help others make meaningful progress, and causes us to overlook the brilliance of those around us. It can ultimately keep us from ever reaching our dreams because we falsely believe we have already arrived.

Chair Stacking

One of the challenges to chasing our ambitions is many of them can't be done alone. Even if they could be, they shouldn't be. Building teams to accomplish our dreams are some of our best opportunities to develop and champion others, but to do it well we must be aware of our current abilities as leaders. We are all better together than we are alone. That's certainly the case when starting a church, and it's true for whatever ambition you're chasing, too. Whether we're building a business, writing a book, or raising our kids, we need the right people at our side. Lacking self-awareness often causes us to miss the fact that the right people are already at our side. It was true for NASA during the race to the moon and true for me at the start of our church.

Our church-planting team was small, but boy did they have talent. If I could have seen it better from the beginning, it would have saved me some gut-wrenching confusion and a little heartache for everyone else.

One of our founding team members, Nii Abrahams, is the owner of a personality with enough energy to launch one of NASA's rockets. Anyone who meets him becomes his friend. If you're relationally challenged or socially awkward, hang with Nii. He'll cover for you.

Another one of our team members, Allie Baughman, is the most wonderfully creative person I know. She manages a clothing boutique during the day. I'm convinced she's a superhero by night. She has impeccable taste, a knack for design, and is quick-thinking and decisive to boot. If you gave me a checklist for the next month, she'd have it done by lunch. No problem.

Nii and Allie aren't the only talented people our team started with. Allie's husband, John, also made the trek to Fishers to start the church with us. He's a brilliant thinker and one of those people whose inner peace and even keel provide calm for those in choppy waters.

John's day job is leading multiple audit teams for an accounting firm called Deloitte. His work is less about bookkeeping than you might imagine and more about managing people. As I would eventually discover, though not as quickly as I could have, he is very, very good at leading people.

In the beginning, I was giving lip service to the idea that I wanted to develop people and discover their potential. I felt that I had accomplished my dream of creating a church that championed people, but I hadn't even gotten started. I thought that I had landed on the moon; in reality I was still firmly on the ground. My lack of self-awareness caused me to focus so much on the vision for the church that I failed to have vision for the people working alongside me. During those days, when I was leading with blinders on, I had incredibly talented people in all the wrong places, doing all the wrong things on Sunday mornings.

My lack of awareness caused me to overlook talented people on my team and kept me from even addressing my first problem—that I didn't know how to build a church where others could discover their God-given potential.

If Nii is awake, people are finding community and realizing that they belong. When it comes to bringing people together, he has the gravitational pull of the sun. I asked him to sing songs.

In a short time under Allie's leadership, the boutique's profits quadrupled. I had her making coffee.

John manages multiple teams of people, some of whom are stationed on the other side of the planet, for four different clients simultaneously. I asked him to stack chairs.

The people on my team would all happily do menial tasks. They aren't the kind of people who believe they are above them. The issue was I *only* had them doing these tasks and wasn't developing them further. Because I lacked self-awareness, people I was passionate about developing weren't growing. Instead of having vision for them, I *only* had vision for the church. Even though I had clear vision for the church, I did not know how to accomplish it. My lack of self-awareness was stunting growth at every level, and I didn't even know it.

I still needed the math to create the necessary trajectory to launch our church, and the people I cared about, into the future God envisioned for us. My lack of awareness concerning my weaknesses as a leader kept me from championing those I love and lead. Worse yet, it caused me to fall headlong into the same trap NASA did in their search for a mathematical genius. I not only failed to develop my team, but I was also overlooking their true worth and selfishly using them only to achieve my dreams.

The Genius Down the Hall

It's hard to explain the brilliance of a mind like the one God gave Katherine Goble. She was the expert in analytic geometry Langley needed—who, by the way, *already worked for them*. Sadly, it's not hard to calculate how Goble flew under NASA's radar. That math has been around for centuries. Racism plus sexism has always equaled blindness to the beauty and potential of others. Her genius should have been easy to locate, no high-powered telescope required, but as we often do as deeply flawed human beings, we choose not to notice because we're crippled by prejudice, massive egos, and at times just plain old stupidity.

These complex issues formed the plot of the inspiring film, *Hidden Figures*, that centered around the lives and struggles of three remarkable black women, Katherine Goble, Dorothy Vaughan, and Mary Jackson.

It's easy to pummel NASA for their sins in overlooking these incredible women. What's more difficult is to examine our own lives and leadership to see what shortcomings are slowing our growth, putting a lid on our success, and doing damage to people we care for and lead.

I had seen the kind of leadership I longed to emulate. Grandpa was a phenomenal example of a leader who used the massive platform he created to accomplish his dream and launch others into theirs. It was easy to spot when others were leading like Grandpa, and incredibly inspiring, but I had not yet discovered how to achieve it on my own.

His vision to share Jesus' love through television was crystal clear, although he was extremely demanding towards those who helped him achieve it. It's important to note, the issue is not *demanding* leadership, it's *selfish* leadership that's the problem.

In the first years of our church-plant, I thought I was leading like Grandpa. I desperately wanted to, but my lack of self-awareness blinded me from seeing that I was slipping into this familiar form of leadership that treats people like pawns. I was becoming someone who overlooked the wonders in those around me, and who couldn't champion others because I was only concerned with whether or not they were championing me.

The Awakening

Waking up from the nightmare of my lack of self-awareness was more of a process than a moment. It was kick-started by my embarrassing two-hour rant chronicled in the previous chapter, but it took a further eighteen months to fully realize to the truth that even though I had clarity on the person and leader I wanted to be, I was currently far from my destination.

What truly opened my eyes to my insecurities and unresolved pain, which were the primary causes of my lack of self-awareness regarding my leadership, was the counseling and coaching I desperately needed. In this season of my life, it was a God-send to have others lovingly show me how far off course I was.

The journey toward the Christ-like leadership I saw in Grandpa is one of incremental gains and often painful setbacks. We never truly arrive there either. The moment we stop growing is the moment we cease to be on the journey with those we love and lead. Becoming the champion of those around you won't happen overnight. It hasn't for me either, but I'm happy we're traveling this road together.

Having my eyes opened to my lack of self-awareness finally allowed me to make two vital improvements. First, to stop overlooking the brilliant and talented people already on my team and finally get them into the right places where their gifts can flourish. Second, to realize that I was like NASA in the 1960s; I had clarity on where I was going, but I did not know how to get there. I was missing the "math" needed to calculate the trajectory that would land me at my dream.

The Math

Watching the 10,000[th] episode of *Huntley Street* inspired me to shoot for the moon. The beauty in Grandpa's visionary leadership was reminiscent of Jesus and ignited a passion in me to champion those who would one day serve alongside me.

I now had clarity on my destination: to be a leader with clear vision for my ministry, but who could also champion the God-given potential and dreams of those I love and lead. That was the brilliant combination Grandpa embodied. What I would soon discover was the "math" that I was missing was the language necessary to clearly communicate this to others and that allowed us to actually accomplish it.

The math I needed to chart the course for our church turned out to be a two-part equation. I discovered the first half while surfing the world wide web. I developed a habit of scouring the website of churches I admired for ideas. This landed me on the homepage of National Community Church, where Mark Batterson is the founding pastor. Clicking on each tab one-by-one, I came across the church's manifesto. That's not a word I had found on anyone else's website. I was intrigued. The manifesto is comprised of a list of desires they have for their church. In the final one I found a description of exactly what I wanted to build at ours. It read:

We hope to become a part of the personal dream God has given you, and we invite you to become a part of the corporate dream God has given us. NCC is a dream factory where people get a vision from God and go for it.[1]

Dreams are a two-way street. For me, that wasn't a revelation. I knew that's what I wanted for our church, but it was the *language I needed to express it well.* One way you can create a place where people can discover their potential is to invite them into the dream God has given you. That was vital for me because I did have a very clear vision for what I felt God was calling me to do, and I needed a lot of people to help me do it. Then, we can hope to be invited to be part of their dreams. Our own God-given dreams and the dreams of our team are not mutually exclusive. No one has to sacrifice what God has for their lives to be a part of our dreams. We don't have to sacrifice ours to be part of theirs. God is big enough for both.

The other half of the equation came from a friend I deeply admire, Bob Goff. Bob was being interviewed by well-known pastor, Craig Groeschel, for his podcast. As they talked about leading people, Bob began to describe his approach. He said that his job is to point to the horizon and tell everyone where they're going.

Then Bob said that he spends no time trying to get anyone on his page. In other words, he's not trying to get everyone to be all about the destination he's pointing toward as a visionary leader. Rather, he spends all his time trying to get the people he leads on *their page.*

He said if the pages go together, then they make the same book. If not, that's no big deal. He works to help them find where their page does fit. Sometimes people had to leave his team because of this, but it's not a bad thing. He can be their biggest fan and help them find where their page does fit. It might be that they need to write their own book.[2]

I now had the exact language I needed to help me understand *how* to lead in a way that helps others discover their potential. We can invite people into the corporate dream we have, and hope they invite us into the personal dreams God has for them.

We can point to the horizon and tell everyone on our staff, in our organization, or on our team where we're headed. We don't have to apologize for it or change it if others don't agree. After laying out our vision for the big ambitions we have, we can spend our time helping others to understand themselves. If we truly want to champion others there is no other option. Leading this way saves us from overlooking the talent all around us. It keeps us from missing the true worth of the people God has placed alongside us. We don't have to sacrifice our dreams, and they don't have to either. Some people will find that being on our team is exactly where they need to be and remain for the long haul. Others will have to move on from our organization to follow their passions. This happened to Grandpa numerous times throughout his career. For him, it wasn't a failure or a setback.

It was his greatest sign of success. It can be ours as well.

If we want to be the champions of those we love and lead self-awareness is vital. The introspection and honesty needed to open our eyes to a lack of awareness in our own lives isn't easy, but it is necessary. Our families, friends, and followers will all be better off if we endure the process.

Nii doesn't lead our worship team anymore. He's our Connections Pastor now. Allie doesn't make coffee anymore. She leads our Events Team and shocks us all with her endless creativity. John still stacks chairs—I think he secretly loves it—he just does it in addition to being our Executive Pastor.

You might dismiss the idea that the Katherine Goble you need is

8

Choose Positivity

WHEN THE UNIVERSITY OF ALABAMA football program hired sports psychologist Trevor Moawad to condition the mental strength of the team, no one could have fathomed how massive his impact would be within the organization.

By his second year working alongside legendary coach Nick Saban, they had narrowed in on one goal for the team:

Stop saying negative things out loud.

That's it. Stop verbalizing all the negative experiences of being on the team.

The reason is simple. Negativity is seventy times more powerful than positivity in terms of its ability to consume our minds and lives, and when something negative is spoken out loud it becomes ten times more powerful than the thought alone.[1]

For the athletes at Alabama, there was enormous pressure to perform. If they didn't measure up quickly, they were cut. The dream of being on the team could end overnight. This pressure created an environment prone to mental anxieties for athletes which, in turn, created fertile ground for the kind of negative thinking that could destroy the whole program.

When players are practicing for the *third* time of the day in the soaring temperatures of an Alabama summer, negativity comes easy. They just want to be done and go home.

Saban and Moawad had fought to build a culture where players *believed* they would win championships—that it was in their DNA—but the outspoken negativity among the team threatened to sabotage the carefully crafted mentality. If negative thinking took root, the team could lose faith in themselves and each other. The result would be disastrous.

Even for those of us who aren't in the charged environment of athletics, we can relate. We experience the anxiety of not being good enough at our jobs and in our relationships. It may not be stifling heat and long days, but we all have things about our circumstances that are fodder for negativity.

Unless we work to banish negativity from our words, we'll lose the opportunity to champion others. When our speech is seasoned by negativity our words lose their appeal. As a gold-medal winning pessimist, I know how taxing it can be to change, but if we want to champion others, it's a battle we must win. It's a war my family and friends want me to wage too; optimistic Jason is way more fun to spend time with.

If we are trying to lead others, but our words are like a pounding rain of negativity, people will eventually move on from us to be cultivated under the influence of someone else.

Those we love and lead deserve someone with a positive outlook to champion them. We don't have to be perfect. If we did, we'd all be out of the race. We just need to be growing, inching our way toward choosing positivity each day.

Engineered for Rain

High above the Sacred Valley in Peru sits one of the new Seven Wonders of the Ancient World; the Incan city of Machu Picchu. It's an architectural and engineering masterpiece. It also receives an annual rainfall of seventy-two inches. More than twice the average for the city of Chicago.

Machu Picchu has stood atop the ridge of its mountain home for more than five centuries enduring torrential rains each year that should have destroyed it, washing it down the mountain and into history.

Mystery abounds at Machu Picchu. Many of its secrets will never be solved, but how the structures have remained in place, despite heavy rains, has been unlocked by researchers. The secret lies just below the surface. It's estimated that as much as sixty percent of the construction for the ancient city is beneath the buildings. Under the center of the city lies a huge base of rock chips, creating a main artery where much of the city's water is channeled away during the rainy season.

Even the famous terraces were not just for farming. They served as a system of filters for funneling the heavy rains down the mountain away from the city. Constructed of a top layer of fertile soil, followed by sandy dirt, and finally a layer of gravel and larger stones, their ingenious design is part of the secret salvation of this ancient wonder.[2]

The builders of Machu Picchu understood that a natural phenomenon outside of their control put what they were building in danger every day. Without the proper substructure to channel the rainwater away, the city wouldn't stand a chance.

In the same way rain could have destroyed Machu Picchu, negativity that wasn't safely channeled away could have brought Nick Saban's legendary success to a screeching halt. It can do the same to the dreams we're working toward, too. Despite Saban's credentials as a coach, the incredible talent they recruit on an annual basis, and the mountain of dollars invested by their donors, they could easily fail to achieve the championships they crave if the team was plagued by a mental weakness born of negative speech.

Moawad understood early on that the onslaught of opportunities to think negatively, and then verbalize those thoughts, was a phenomenon he couldn't control. It's not possible to create a sports program that slams the door on negativity. That's not how life works in football or in our families, let alone our workplaces, classrooms, friendships, or churches. What we need is a system beneath the surface that safely channels negativity away, leaving what we are attempting to build—a positive outlook and a voice others are eager to listen to—intact.

A Lonely World

I have a bad habit of verbalizing negative thoughts. I even have a favorite spot for it—driving alone in the car. I slip into cycles of thinking through situations, and often the people involved, that frustrate me. I fume as I list grievances over and over. It is a record that needs to be broken. Unfortunately, the turntable is often in good working order.

Alone in the car, the need for diplomacy disappears, so I can let the sour rhetoric soar. During a particularly difficult season, I noticed how toxic my diatribes were getting, but I kept venting anyway.

At the time, I convinced myself that my behavior mirrored Abraham Lincoln's. He was viciously attacked by his detractors—and there were many—throughout his presidency. At times, Lincoln would sit down and scribble out scathing rebuttals to his critics, then leave them unsigned and unsent.

I believed I was just doing my own version of what Lincoln did. But there is a big difference. I didn't write my thoughts out once, toss them in the back of a desk, and forget they ever existed. Lincoln vented and moved on with the important work of unifying a nation. I kept reciting outloud the defeating and depressing thoughts to myself repeatedly. Far from letting the negativity flow away, I was pooling it up, and diving deeper into despair.

Loneliness was my only companion. Of course, that wasn't true, but that's how it felt. When our team moved to the Indianapolis area to help us start the church, everyone had to get jobs outside the church. There was only funding for one employee, which at first was me, so I worked alone all day, every day. For some, like my amazing wife, that's not a problem at all. She prefers it at times. Then again, she's also a super-hero so it's not a fair comparison.

Working in isolation was part of what led me to spiral downward into one of the darkest seasons of my life. Constantly verbalizing everything that made my situation difficult was another. The worst part was that I was becoming a person I never wanted to be: someone whose negativity makes his presence undesirable.

I was becoming a Debby Downer, the infamous Saturday Night Live character brought to life by comedian Rachel Dratch, who was famously and hilariously negative about everything. Her down-in-the-dumps approach makes must-watch television but is terrible in real life. During that season, I steered every conversation back around to my pain. Help abounded in a host of people who cared deeply for me, but I didn't want to heal. I wanted to complain. Sometimes, we desire pity more than hope. It's awful, and it's exactly where I was.

Instead of drawing people close, my negativity repelled them. I was trying to be someone who saw the potential in others and helped them cultivate it. Building an *entire church* that would take up that mantle was my greatest passion. But loneliness and isolation were leading me into an increasingly pessimistic outlook and approach to leadership. Negativity was threatening to destroy the influence I had carefully cultivated in the lives of those I loved and led.

I had spent years developing relationships and convincing people they truly are a masterpiece designed by God. That was my greatest joy in life. But I was like Machu Picchu without the substructure. My influence was being carried away in the mudslides caused by the downpour of negativity that was stealing my focus in life. I used to think I couldn't be positive because of my circumstances. I thought the situation had to change in order to renew my outlook. During that season, I discovered that I must work toward choosing positivity, but the way forward was a mystery I had yet to unravel.

If we don't choose positivity, we can't focus on the beauty in people all around us—we will inevitably make life about ourselves. Negativity turns our lives increasingly inward until we're consumed with ourselves. In multiple seasons of life, I could have been the spokesperson for this condition.

If you're still wondering, can negativity really be that destructive? The answer is unequivocally, *yes.*

War Against Hope

It is a strange fact of history that the most effective prisoner of war camps had no brick walls or barbed wire fences; no towers with guards posted twenty-four hours a day with rifles at the ready. There were no beatings or floggings either. The prisoners could easily have walked away at any time. They never did. Not a single escape was even attempted.

The North Koreans who created these camps devised a far more sinister method than the brutality normally associated with prison camps. They employed a scheme of psychological warfare to take away one thing from their prisoners—*hope*.

The guards rewarded prisoners for betraying one another. This system created a culture where soldiers routinely turned on each other, causing them to lose trust in their fellow captives, creating a feeling of isolation and loneliness rather than the unbreakable devotion common among prisoners in POW camps.

So much of what is beautiful about our existence, the bonds of friendship, the security of loving relationships, and hope for the future, were stripped from the prisoners with devastating psychological effect.

The mental warfare waged by the North Korean captors was more effective at imprisoning people than walls and bullets. Food was plentiful at the camps, but captured soldiers were starved of reasons to hope. Their minds were swirling with destructive thinking. They broke their prisoners' minds, and their spirits soon followed. It was not uncommon for a soldier to walk into his hut, sit down on the ground, pull his blanket over his head and give up. He would be dead within two days.[3]

Most of us have never been in a situation anywhere near what the soldiers in the Korean War experienced behind enemy lines. The only comparison for us is that a negative thought-life can be like a prison without walls or guards with guns. We could leave the prison of negative thinking at any time, we just don't believe we can. So, we don't. Our situation doesn't need to change. Our choice needs to change. It won't be easy, but we must take charge of what we think and when we think it. The first step is to stop saying negative things outloud.

I still work alone, but now I fight to surround myself with positive, life-giving people as often as I can. I even take trips to visit them from time to time. If we're going to win the battle with verbalizing our negative thoughts, the first thing we will need is good friends.

Good friends are those who possess an unwavering belief in us and who are very good at convincing us that we're more able and successful than we feel. Spending time with them enables us to be more gracious towards ourselves, and our perceived lack of progress. Spend all the time you can with them. When you can't make the drive to be together, make a call, or Facetime with them. Surround yourself with those who challenge you to stop speaking lies and who fill your mind with positive and uplifting words of affirmation.

To gain ground in my battle with negativity, I also had to develop a new habit for when I'm driving alone. Now, rather than verbalizing destructive thoughts—*which makes them ten times more powerful than the thoughts alone*—I listen to podcasts. Not just random ones. As a part of choosing positivity, I choose to listen to episodes by people whose adversity in life far exceeds my own, but who have themselves chosen positivity. I've listened to several of them numerous times. My all-time favorite is an interview with Joni Eareckson Tada, who despite being a quadriplegic, and battling relentless chronic pain, has consistently chosen positivity and joy.

She decided that in order to stave off consuming depression and debilitating negativity she would devote her life to helping others find hope and healing. She has a lot of great friends around her to help. She fills her mind not only with their voices, but with Scripture, too. She verbalizes God's words instead of hopeless thoughts and negative lies.

Her suffering, and the astonishing way she has navigated it for decades, has given her words remarkable weight. Every word she speaks has power. But if she had chosen to be overwhelmed by negativity—as she so easily could have—it would have made her circumstance incomparably worse and cost her the ability to inspire millions of people.

We may not have traveled the same path in life as Joni, but we are all faced with our own version of her choice. How we decide to navigate our circumstances will determine whether we cultivate influence and use it to help others, or wallow in self-pity and a woe-is-me mentality. We can choose negativity and use our voices to speak lifeless thoughts alone in the car or we can choose positivity and raise our voices with a hope and joy.

Choose the right people to be around, then make the call, the drive, or the flight if you must. Like Joni, make your life about helping others find victory in suffering and hope in the midst of pain.

Habits like choosing the right friends, filling our minds with positive and life-giving voices, or helping others who are hurting are how we inch toward choosing positivity more consistently. Over time, these habits become the substructure that can channel away destructive thinking, allowing the influence and relationships we've built to flourish.

Like Alabama's football program, we can stop saying negative things out loud, and curb its power to effect how we lead. When it comes to the secondary step of banishing negative thoughts the solutions won't be the same for every person because the causes aren't universal. For some, professional counseling will be necessary, and for others medical treatment will be a part of the solution. All of us will need good people around us, God's help, and a commitment to choose positivity. With the right people in our corner, we can begin the journey away from the captivity brought on by a destructive thought life.

Our lives can be focused on others and discovering the wonders waiting within those we love and lead. To get there, we must curb negative speech, and create a system to channel away the negative thoughts that can corrode our character. Choosing positivity isn't easy—it will take deliberate work, and help from Jesus and our other good friends, but if we truly want to champion others it's the only path.

PART III

The Way Forward

"Motivation is what gets you started. Habit is what keeps you going."[1]

Jim Ryun

HABIT 1

Learn Who They Are

9

The Journalist's Mindset

AT THE DAWN OF THE twentieth century, J. D. Rockefeller was the richest man on earth. His sprawling empire, Standard Oil, controlled 75% of all the oil in America and wielded incredible influence over the economy and the government. His fortune, translated into today's value, is estimated to be in excess of 400 billion dollars. More than the wealth of Bill Gates, Jeff Bezos, and Warren Buffett combined.

At the height of his success, Rockefeller seemed untouchable, until an investigative journalist named Ida Tarbell, a woman small in stature, but fearless in her hunt for the truth, brought Standard Oil to its knees.

Rockefeller attempted to bury the story before it could be exposed. Prior to Tarbell's investigation, he had scoured the country and purchased every printed piece of material containing negative information about himself or his company—he burned them all. Despite his efforts, Tarbell's intrepid journalism eventually unearthed the corruption behind Rockefeller's rise to dominance.

Her dogged determination would break up Standard Oil's monopoly, lead to the creation of the Federal Trade Commission, and inspire legislation designed to curtail the corrupt practices of America's largest companies. At a time when she wasn't even allowed to vote, Tarbell toppled a titan. Her perseverance to uncover the truth became the standard for investigative reporting. To this day, journalists stand on the foundation her work established.

Stories serve as the currency of journalism. Without them, there is nothing to report and no job for reporters. We may not be journalists, but if we truly want to discover the potential in others, we must adopt the way they think. So, at our church we ask all our leaders to go into every environment in search of a story. We call it *the journalist's mindset.*

To discover the potential of those around us, we must learn to ask more questions and make fewer statements. To champion others effectively, we must learn who they are. Great questions create opportunities for us to see deeper into the lives of those we love and lead. Making statements allows others to understand us but will keep us from our goal of learning about them. Questions are one of our most effective tools for discovery. Ida Tarbell made it an artform. To reveal the unseen God-given potential in others, it's a skill we will have to master.

Reverse Mentoring

When the opportunity came to have lunch with Dr. Earl Creps, I was a little intimidated. I quickly realized I didn't need to be. His towering intellect is more than matched by a disarming warmth that stems from his genuine interest in others. Despite my uneasy feeling, I was excited to meet with a theologian and author of his stature. In a lot of ways, he was someone I wanted to emulate. I figured I was in for a good lunch and a rare chance to peer into the mind of a great thinker. I am certain there were brilliant thoughts bouncing around Earl's mind but leaving lunch that day I didn't know what any of them were.

We had only met briefly before, and in the introductory phase of our lunch Earl found out I was someone who preached at various events, including week-long summer youth camps. He had recently been invited to speak at one and was intimidated by the opportunity because it was outside his comfort zone of the classroom.

For the rest of our time together he peppered me with questions about how I handle these events. No detail was insignificant. He wanted to know everything I knew. I was happy to oblige. It wasn't until after our lunch was over that I fully realized that Earl had flipped the script on me. I went into lunch eager to learn from a brilliant man whose knowledge of the Bible far surpassed my own, but Earl found an area of life where he considered me the expert and homed in on it with surgical precision asking one question after another.

I went into lunch impressed by his genius, but because of his genuine interest and skill at asking great questions, I left feeling like I was the one who was brilliant. I have come to find that Earl calls this reverse mentoring and that he does it all the time. It certainly left an impression on me I'll never forget.

In our mission to add value to those around us, to help them understand their inherent worth as God's creation, and find their purpose and fulfill God-given dreams, we have to become great at asking questions like Ida and Earl. Making statements and sharing stories of our own has its place for sure. But we have to keep in mind there is beauty buried deep within those we're championing, and it will only come to light when we take the time to see their souls, hear their hurts, and mine for the wonders waiting within them by crafting well-aimed questions.

Attentiveness

When Jesus interacted with the crowds, miracles were commonplace. That's why he had to get up in the middle of the night to have a moment to himself. Wherever he went the crowds were sure to follow. People longed to be near Jesus.

It wasn't just because he told great stories and spoke with authority, though he did. The astonishing healings of the blind and lame contributed too. But there was a constant miracle Jesus performed that is underappreciated because it often flies below our radar:

Jesus made people feel valued.

He did it in the most unassuming way—by asking questions. This habit allowed him to give people the gift of *attention*.

Our need for attention is the opening subject of one of my favorite books, *Revolutionary Communicator*. I have reread the first

THE JOURNALIST'S MINDSET 103

chapter, *Attentiveness*, countless times. It shaped my life early on in my ministry career. In the book, authors Jedd Medefind and Eric Lokkesmoe convincingly make the case that humanity has a universal and desperate need: attention.

We all long to be noticed by others; to have the eager, warm, compassionate, eyes of another truly see us for who we are. Mother Teresa said lacking attention in this way is the greatest form of human suffering. A subject in which she was well versed.[1] I don't like to admit it most of the time, you may not either, but we all long for this gift. We all deeply want to be seen and celebrated, valued and understood. Jesus was the undisputed master at finding those who needed this the most, and providing it in abundant, life-changing, supply.

Seen and Heard

One of Jesus' most well-known miracles involved healing a blind man named Bartimaeus. The day Jesus was in town, the people of Jericho were particularly dismissive and repeatedly tried to silence him as he cried out for Jesus' attention. In a way Ida Tarbell would have admired, Bartimaeus didn't relent. He just shouted louder.

Jesus halted the crowd and asked for Bartimaeus to come to him. The blind man ran to Jesus. Imagine that scene for a moment. It seems reckless for a blind man to run, but because Jesus was the one calling to him, I think it would have been more reckless to do anything else.

Jesus leaned toward Bartimaeus and asked a question, "What do you want me to do for you?".[2] Everyone knew the answer. So why ask? Because Jesus understood beyond his sight being restored, there was a more profound need to be met in that moment. Bartimaeus was starved for attention. That day was not the first time people ignored him. That likely happened with frightening regularity. Yes, he wanted to see, but Jesus understood that Bartimaeus, like all of us, wanted to *be seen* even more.

This moment is a beautiful example of what it must have felt like to be around Jesus. He wasn't adored just for the eye-popping miracles. He was the master at creating moments for people to feel seen and valued. Jesus wasn't beloved only for his divine ability to raise the dead, but for his human capacity to raise the still-breathing to new life.

By asking them questions.

Questions aren't just about the stories they can bring to light. Even if we know the answer, they are still worth asking because of the worth they convey to others. Living each day with a journalist mindset allows us to understand those we are championing at a deeper level. It also creates moments for miracles. People all around us are desperate to be seen and understood; to be valued by being listened to. It's what Earl did for me at our lunch meeting. He made me feel brilliant and capable because he asked me questions. He was genuinely interested in me and what I knew. It may be a minor miracle compared to Bartimaeus receiving his sight, but it's a miracle none-the-less. It's one that can be repeated in the lives of those we love and lead if we will ask more questions and make fewer statements.

Who can you call over to you? Who can you give a seat at the table? The next time we meet with those we mentor, what if we reverse the script and allow them to teach us by asking more questions? They might leave feeling like we're the expert because we share our knowledge and experience, but they could leave understanding there is more brilliance in them than they have imagined if we will listen to them. If you really want to show them their value, rather than asking them to record your advice, take out a notebook and write down what *they say*. That's what Earl did for me that day. I couldn't believe he thought what I was saying was worth writing down.

We are quick to offer our advice and share what we've learned with those we are championing, and that has its place, but often we are too slow to ask questions, give opportunities, and show others how valuable they truly are by listening. You can listen more at bedtime with your kids, to your students in the classroom, or on the drive home with your spouse. It will not only help them feel seen and valued, it will help you understand them. Until we do, we cannot truly champion them. Adopt the mindset of a journalist. Call someone over to you and ask a great question. It will not only help you learn who they are but might well be the beginning of the healing they need.

A Simple Question

This book is the result of a question. I had no plan to ask it. It turned out to be the right question aimed at the right person—my friend, John Baughman.

John is the ultimate teammate. He's a better-than-average basketball player, but if you find yourself on the court with him even one time, you'll quickly notice a pattern. He lives to pass the ball. He would rather get you the ball so you can take the winning shot than keep the opportunity for himself. John wants to celebrate you, not be celebrated by you.

One summer, John and I were on a short trip together. We were killing time at the hotel reading books and being lazy when I became more curious about a question than the story I was reading. I closed the book, and asked John, "If you could do anything at Parkside, just write your own job description, what would you do?"

He thought briefly and said, "I would want to lead our leaders." If John had stopped there, this book might not have been written.

He went on to explain what he meant, saying, "I want them to know I'm in their corner. I want to help them grow and get better and be their cheerleader to help them succeed." With a slight rise of emotion evident in his voice, John finished, saying, "I want to be there when they fall down, help them get back up again, and keep going."

For the record, when most people talk about leading other leaders, that is not at all what they mean. I would discover it over and over in the years to come, but on that day with striking clarity, I was beginning to see how extraordinary John really is.

I didn't know it at the time, but that question was a defining moment in my life and leadership. It was the beginning of a new journey for John and me and for the organization we lead. John wanted to be *everyone's biggest fan.* He lives to help the team, and each individual, hit the winning shot, and then act like he had nothing to do with their victory. It's who he was made to be.

Now it's who we're all trying to be.

Before my conversation with John, I knew God was calling our church to be a place where people could discover and fulfill their God-given potential. In the language of author Simon Sinek, it's our "just cause," the reason we exist. What I didn't have a handle on is how to do it. Asking John a good question led to an integral part of the answer I was desperately searching for. The way you create an organization that helps people find their potential is to create a leadership culture where everyone is required to use their influence and authority the way Jesus would: *for the benefit of everyone but themselves.*

What people like Ida and my friend Earl have been teaching me is that asking questions is a powerful way to shift our focus away from ourselves and toward those we love and lead. Asking John that question not only helped me discover an incredible piece of his potential, it changed my life and how I lead.

That's the power of a question.

Revelations

The impact of asking John one question will stretch through generations because it now shapes how I parent and pastor. I want to be the biggest fan of those I love and lead. I hope you do too. We'll need Ida Tarbell's tenacity, Earl's wisdom, and the compassion and patience of Jesus to call others over to us, listen to their stories, and ultimately add value to their lives. It will be worth it, not only for their sake, but for ours. Living to discover the God-given potential within others is the most enjoyable way to live, and like Jesus, it will make us the most enjoyable people to be around.

Even though my kids are still young, I love to ask them questions. The answers may not be life-changing, but they are often hilarious. Laughter really is great medicine. God knows every parent needs it to make up for the lack of sleep. One night at dinner a friend asked my son Declan what he wanted to do with his life. He was four at the time. As his eyes narrowed and the corners of his mouth formed a coy smile he whispered, "*Dangerous things.*"

We all lost it.

I am committed to giving them opportunities to discover their incredible potential by asking better questions. I still have plenty of things to say, and I plan on saying them repeatedly. After all, I'm a parent and repeating yourself is part of the job, but I'm learning to ask first, listen second, and speak third.

Whether you own a business, lead a church, or are a stay-at-home parent, championing others is more attainable than we imagine. It starts with a holy curiosity about what God has placed in every person—digging for that treasure with the deceptively simple tool of asking questions.

There is no way to know what's on the other side of the right question until it's asked. I hope you fall in love with that mystery. I hope you fall in love with finding the wonders waiting in every person. Go into every situation with a journalist's mindset. Whether you're interacting with those you revere or someone you've just met, be their cheerleader and coach for a moment by asking better questions. There's no telling what you might discover.

10

Friend

AT THE AGE OF THIRTEEN, Joe arrived home to a confusing sight: his
father and stepmother were putting his little brothers into the back
of the family car. Joe noticed that the car was also packed with
luggage. His father told him the family's meager income was no
longer enough to provide for both him and his younger half-
brothers, so they were moving to a place where hopefully his father
would find higher paying work. It was a scene played out countless
times during the Great Depression.

The memory of the car pulling away as he stood in the driveway,
stunned, would remain with him for the rest of his life. Even in his
later years he could hear little Harry sobbing and screaming
repeatedly, "*What about Joe? What about Joe?*"[1]

Joe Rantz was now alone in the world.

This moment would send Joe on a journey not only to find food
and shelter, but to find value as a person after being abandoned by
his family. Understandably, he would struggle to feel wanted for
years to come.

It wasn't until he enrolled at the University of Washington and joined the rowing team that Joe would find his value again. The boys in the boat with him would defy all odds and become Olympic champions.

However, Joe's feelings of worth didn't come from being a winner (though I'm sure winning gold would make most of us feel pretty great for a moment at least), they came from the fact that his teammates were his *friends* and that they wanted to be in the boat with him.

The people who helped Joe Rantz rediscover his value as a human being were just a rag-tag bunch of boys from the Pacific Northwest. They weren't experts in psychology or therapists who specialized in the kind of trauma Joe experienced watching his family drive away. They were just friends. As is often the case for those of us trying to discover our worth, that's all Joe needed them to be.

For the people we are championing, that's all they need us to be.

Titles

In our search for meaning and value we often reach for the wrong sources. We live in a world where people are obsessed with titles because they can convey a certain worth for those who hold them. In recent times, the titles have become increasingly over-the-top and ridiculous. A quick online search will yield a litany of amusing job descriptions in the corporate world. Many of them, unsurprisingly, are at tech companies.

In today's culture, the person in charge of the website development is now the "*Digital Overlord.*" At Microsoft, the employee in charge of marketing is now the "*Chief Storyteller*". Google employs an "*In-House Philosopher,*" tasked with using a humanist perspective to solve engineering problems. Whatever that means.

If you watch the credits scroll by for long enough, you'll discover that one person needed to make the film *Indiana Jones and the Last Crusade*, one of my all-time favorite films, was a "*Creature Supervisor.*" Which could also be an alternate title for parent.

Sometimes companies are tired of the old descriptions for what people do and are just having fun with these titles, but often we work toward achieving these kinds of labels because it's a way of feeling more important. When we feel unwanted, abandoned, or rejected we search to regain our value. Joe rediscovered his in a group of teammates who became his brothers, but sometimes the longing for self-worth leads us to chase positions of prominence or titles like *president, chairman*, or *CEO*. It could be *professor, doctor, owner*, or being labeled as "*successful*" or a "*winner*" by others. This is tempting not because these labels matter to us, but because they mean so much to everyone else. We don't really long for fancy titles or letters behind our name. It is what they represent that we're after. It's the respect of our peers, the admiration from followers, and the applause of others that can make us feel that we have value. That's what we truly crave.

Teacher

Jesus had a title while he was here on earth—*Teacher*. In that day, the position Jesus held was highly respected and the students who followed these instructors closely often referred to them as "*Master*." (Not sure why more people in Silicon Valley haven't worked that into their job titles.) It was also common in Jesus' day for those who followed a particular teacher to be referred to as "*servants*".

That's what makes the title Jesus gave his closest followers all the more bewildering. He broke tradition—which in his culture was more of a fatal error than a faux pas. Jesus explained to his followers that having a relationship with him was like a vine and its branches. To be separated from him meant they would wither away. Without him, Jesus was saying, there is *no life*. In that same moment Jesus conferred upon them a new title, a new way of knowing and being known. He told them they would no longer be called his servants because they knew him and were connected to him.[2]

Now, he said, they would be called his *friends*.

Most of us would love to have a title that elevates our sense of importance, but is friend a title capable of this feat? Is it a label that encompasses great significance for us in terms of how others see us and how we value ourselves?

According to Jesus, the answer is *yes*.

It's time for us to revisit the power of being called a friend. Jesus knew what he was doing when he told his disciples—who definitely were his servants—that he would call them friends instead. Jesus didn't give them a title he believed was second best. He wasn't holding back.

Jesus believed friend was the best title he could give.

It bears remembering Jesus was explaining to his closest followers that knowing him *was life itself*. That's the incomparable worth of Jesus. He was using the metaphor of a vine and its branches to convey it. Then Jesus shifted from speaking about his own value to talking about ours. He wanted to reveal to those he loved and led what their worth was to him: and so he called them friends.

In Jesus' eyes, our worth can be conveyed in that one word.

If you want to champion people and help them discover and achieve the potential God has placed inside of them then it's the only title you'll ever need.

If you have a position of authority, that's a great bonus. If you're someone's teacher, coach, boss, or pastor, that's not a bad or irrelevant thing. Those extra titles add dimensions of influence that can be helpful, but at the end of the day if we were stripped of all of them, as long as we are someone's friend, then we can be an integral part of helping those we lead become who God made them to be.

In fact, the more you matter in the mind of someone else the less time you need to change his or her life. I remember a moment I met someone I deeply admired. We spoke for only a short time, but I can quote what he said to me verbatim. He probably forgot about the conversation by the end of the day. Not because he's a bad person, but because he had conversations with countless people like me that day. My admiration for him gave the words he spoke an incredible weight.

We might have influence as a person of prominence who is well-known and widely respected. We also may have a voice in the lives of those around us as a boss, teacher, or pastor. Even being a parent doesn't guarantee we'll have a voice in the lives of those we love the most, but being their friend does. Whatever roles we may have in the lives of others, friend is the most important title we can have because it allows us to authentically champion, lead, and love those around us so that they can reach their God-given potential.

The Music of Life

I visit the same coffee shop several times a week. It's my favorite place to write and dream about the future. I've been going there for months now, and Elijah takes my order every time—I've started to wonder if maybe he lives there. Elijah writes music and has a band. I only know this because he told me not long after I started coming in regularly. The following week, I came in at my usual time, and as soon as he saw me, he said, "I want you to listen to my song." I thought, "I just came to get a cup of coffee," but told him I'd be happy to. It was pretty good! These days, Elijah knows quite a bit about me, and I know about his ambition to do music full time someday, and what new members he's added to his band, and some random things about his family's Christmas traditions. Elijah shares a lot about his life.

From the first time I met him, Elijah never saw me as a potential customer but as a potential friend. We talk almost every day now, sharing about our lives and dreams. He talks about his music. I talked with him a lot about this book. These days, my coffee comes with a lot of encouragement because of Elijah. His optimism is contagious.

He's a young man with his whole life ahead of him. I offer advice from time to time, and return the encouragement. Even though he doesn't attend my church I also have plenty of pastoral things to say to him, but the reason I have a voice in his life at all is because he saw me as his friend. Elijah doesn't just know me, he knows everyone who comes through the door, and no matter who they are he treats everyone with the same warmth and openness. After all, whomever they may be, whatever labels or titles life has heaped upon them, good or bad, to Elijah, they are just potential friends.

What I've realized is that Elijah sees people a lot like Jesus did. Jesus never gave much thought to how society viewed others. Luke chapter five describes an encounter Jesus had with a tax-collector named Levi. In that culture, collecting taxes meant he was a traitor to his own people, taking their money to appease corrupt and wicked rulers. A special brand of hatred was reserved for tax-collectors, but when Jesus met Levi, even though everyone else despised him, Jesus saw him as his friend.[3]

The ability to see past the labels society has burdened someone with, to look beyond their past, their fears, and their façade to immediately see them as a friend allows us to learn who they truly are. Much like Elijah's music, every life is a song worth listening to. If we cannot genuinely know those we are called to lead, and begin to understand them, we will never be able to champion them. Seeing people as Jesus did saves us from ever seeing them as just a customer, a client, or a commodity. Jesus never saw his disciples this way. Even when they failed miserably at following his teachings in humiliating fashion, he saw them as people to be loved, not problems to be solved. He saw their true worth at first sight, because he saw them from the beginning as his friends. Whether the people we love and lead are members of our family, a new addition to our band, or an old neighbor we have tried hard to ignore, we must learn to see them as Jesus would. As a person longing to be known, loved, and believed in—as someone who needs us to be their friend.

Longboards and Board Games

My buddy Andy has taught me a lot about the power of friendship. He leads a campus ministry called Chi Alpha at Missouri State University in Springfield, MO, and in the years he has been there hundreds of students have experienced his leadership. If they were each asked to describe him using a single word, I bet nearly everyone would choose the same one: friend.

For most of these Chi Alpha students Andy is not their first pastor, but for many, he's their favorite. Andy is a master at figuring out what matters to people and then experiencing it alongside them. He doesn't try to convince them to jump in on what's important to him. If he did, he would miss his opportunity to learn who they are. Also, they'd all just be playing disc golf constantly and helping him carry his egregiously large backpack full of discs. Andy doesn't try to get everyone on his turf or on his terms. He figures out their passions and what matters to them. It's a vital component of being someone's friend and learning who they are.

There was a student who was in a rough place who loved to longboard. Andy had never longboarded before, and if you know Andy you know he has no business trying as someone who has severely injured himself while *bowling*, but none of that matters to him. He bought a longboard and started spending time with that student. It was the beginning of a whole new life for that young man. For Andy, it was just another day at the office as the *Chief of Friendship* at MO State Chi Alpha. I think his real title is "*Director*", but he should change it, or at least figure out how to incorporate "*Master*" into it.

It's not just longboards. Andy will play basketball or nerdy board games with people often until the middle of the night, or go to pageants or plays to watch them perform. When Andy spends time with you there is no clock, no limit, and no agenda. There is just you and his passion to discover your true worth. Andy knows how to make people feel valued and wanted. He's a master at it. We could come up with some absurd title for having that role in people's lives but Jesus already did it perfectly when he called us his friends.

Every one of us can be a little more like Andy. It doesn't require a degree and doesn't have a giant learning curve. Too often we think making a difference in people's lives requires a status of some kind which leads us down an unfortunate path of trying to discover our self-importance in the wrong places. It also makes life about us, not about others. The exact opposite of Jesus.

It will require us to open our eyes to the reality that there are scores of people like Joe Rantz all around us, longing to be valued again. We need to learn who they are, and pray we are invited into their lives. We will also have to integrate our lives with Jesus more, so that when the invitations come, we are ready to be a healing presence and a voice of hope for them. Even if that means we have to learn to longboard. We must search for our true worth in Jesus, not in the titles and positions life may offer us. Then we will be free to make our lives all about others and the wonders waiting within them.

There is part of me that still longs for some of the other labels our world thinks are important, but because of the influence of people like Andy and Elijah, and a lot of help from Jesus, I'm learning that friend is the only title we really need.

HABIT 2

Love Who They Are

11

Higher!

MILTON WRIGHT LOVED WORDS.

As a bishop whose career in ministry spanned five decades, he spoke them constantly. As an avid reader, he devoured them. Both he and his wife, Catherine, enjoyed learning for its own sake and surrounded themselves with words. Their home in Dayton, OH, had two libraries. A rare luxury in those days. The first was reserved for works of theology, the other was filled with books on a wide variety of interests.[1]

The Wright's passion for learning and well stocked libraries created a welcoming environment for both imagination and investigation. It was the perfect setting for a spark of interest in a particular subject to be fanned into a lasting flame.

The Wright's passion for learning allowed two of their sons, known as "Will" and "Orv", to dream of human flight and to foster that dream into a reality that would change history and open the world to travel like never before.

Huffman Prairie

From our schooling, most of us remember that the first human flight on a powered aircraft took place in Kittyhawk, NC, on December, 17, 1903. Onboard the *Wright Flyer*, Wilbur piloted the powered glider for a twelve second flight covering a whopping one hundred and twenty feet. Less than the wingspan of a Boeing 747. It was long enough, though, to classify as the first ever flight. What is less commonly recalled is that the place Orville and Wilbur truly proved their theory of controlled flight, eventually staying aloft for hours at a time, was an eighty-four acre property just outside of Dayton, OH, called Huffman Prairie.

This unassuming field is also the place where Bishop Milton Wright would speak some of the best words of his life. The message he shared one eventful day at Huffman was only three words long. It wasn't a sermon, and it wasn't preached from a pulpit. It was shouted from an airplane to an audience of one, his youngest son. Orville would remember his father's words for the rest of his life. It was the right message delivered in the right moment, and it contained the incredible combination of encouragement *and* challenge.

If we truly want to help those we love and lead achieve their full potential we will have to learn this artform from Milton Wright. We must fall in love with words and learn to use them to both encourage people by recognizing how far they've come, and challenge them to take risks, dream bigger, and continue growing.

After a lifetime of practice, Milton could embody all of this in only three words.

Three Words

When the Huffman family bought a plot of land eight miles northeast of Dayton, OH, they possessed no hints of its future significance. The eighty plus acres of rough prairie grass would become the place human beings mastered the art of flying an airplane and the site of the world's first airport and first school for pilots. I was excited when the opportunity to visit Huffman Prairie came. I had no idea being there would inspire how I try to parent my three children, pastor my church, and lead those I love.

By the fall of 1910, the Wright brothers had been flying for about six-and-a-half years. Their flying machine and the ability to pilot it had been tested time and again. On May 25th of that year, two firsts took place at Huffman Prairie. Orville and Wilbur had promised their father they would never fly together. Having lost two children in infancy, he couldn't handle the thought of losing two more in a plane crash. That day, Milton relented, and the boys climbed aboard and flew together. And then their father, at the age of eighty-one, sat down next to his youngest son, Orville, and took flight for the first time in what must have been a magical experience for him.

There is a sign at Huffman Prairie commemorating Milton's flight. An excerpt from Tom Crouch's biography of the Wright brothers is quoted on it. It recounts the moment that would stay with Orville for the rest of his life. During the flight, Milton leaned toward his son, and shouted above the rumble of the engine, the whirr of the propellors, and the swoosh of the slipstream, three words that were etched into Orville's mind forever:

"Higher, Orville, higher!"[2]

Statistically speaking, as an octogenarian, Milton Wright had spoken half a billion words in his lifetime. I would argue, this mid-flight call to Orville were three of his best.

If we want to see those we love and lead flourish and succeed, we will have to learn the secret power of Milton's words that day. They were a brilliant combination of what is necessary to empower others to fulfill their God-given potential.

In one word, *"higher"*, Milton recognized what his sons had already accomplished. He couldn't make the call to ascend to a new height if they weren't already in the air. He acknowledged all his sons had worked toward up to that point. They had imagined an airplane then built and tested it time and again at great risk and expense. They had persevered through setbacks; through daunting and dangerous challenges until they finally succeeded. They not only created an airplane, they mastered how to fly it safely. At this crowning moment, using the same word again, *"higher"*, Milton called his son to go further, to keep learning, and keep dreaming. It was a precise combination of words offered in the perfect moment. Orville walked with the gift of those encouraging and challenging words for the rest of his days.

The Power Combo

I love that Orville's inspirational moment with his father was totally unplanned. I think these moments happen for all of us. If we live with heightened awareness, we can be a part of creating inspiration for each other more regularly.

One night I was walking through a dark parking lot following a conference I attended when a car pulled up next to me. The tinted window slowly rolled down. Thankfully, it turned out to be two of my favorite people, Greg and Shaylyn Ford. They asked if I had eaten dinner, which was strange, since it was ten o'clock at night. I already had but said I would be happy to join them at whatever place was still open in nearby Waxahachie, TX.

It turns out, that place was a Perkins restaurant. If it weren't for my love for the Fords, that would have been a dealbreaker. I'd rather eat at a gas station, frankly.

Our conversation quickly turned to church and leadership as it often does, since we pastor churches. I told them that we had an amazing team of people but that I was struggling to help them achieve what I knew they were capable of as leaders. Not only at church, but in life.

Greg then told me about a survey he had done with his staff. It was an informal questionnaire to find out what kind of leadership people had flourished under at different times in their lives.

In the responses to the survey questions a common theme emerged. What they found, to their surprise, was that almost everyone talked about the same kind of leader in their lives.

Whether it was a coach, a teacher, a pastor, or a parent, they all described essentially the same thing about the impact those leaders had on their lives.

Those leaders believed in them without fail and were an incredible source of encouragement. Those same leaders were also the ones who challenged them the most, called out their complacency, and pushed them to keep going and growing.

The leaders that caused people to grow possessed both the ability to encourage *and* challenge at the same time.

The three words Milton shouted into Orville's ear contained that brilliant mixture. Milton's call to go higher both acknowledged what the brothers had already achieved, the ability to safely build and fly an airplane, but also pushed them to keep going.

I didn't know when I was consuming a mediocre meal at Perkins that I would get a revelation about leadership, but I should have expected it in hindsight. It's actually a fairly common occurrence when hanging out with the Ford's.

Encouragement toward those we love is essential, but so is calling them to go higher. The power is all in the combination. Either one without the other is drastically less effective. If our goal is to champion others and help them discover all that God has made them to be, then we've got to cultivate a leadership that encourages people by acknowledging how far they've come, and also propels them to chase bigger ambitions than ever before.

Insults and Inspiration

I'm not sure how many things we remember from when we were thirteen. I'm not sure how much we should remember. Wearing braces and being rejected by our peers aren't exactly memories we need to tote around for the long haul.

I don't have a scientific study to back this up, but my guess is we remember a lot of things that essentially fall into one of two categories: insults and inspiration.

We remember the best and the worst. For whatever reason, we remember the negative with far more ease, but when something is truly inspiring or encouraging it can stay with us forever.

One night several of my friends and I were hanging out at the home of our pastor at the time, Lowell Perkins. No relation to the restaurant, thankfully.

I don't recall what was said, but my pastor made a joke about one of us and we all laughed. Then my friend Mike said that Lowell should say something nice about each of us to make up for poking fun at our friend.

Mike didn't know he had set the stage for a moment I would never forget.

Lowell gladly accepted the challenge. I have no idea what he said to anyone else that night, but when he got to me, he said, "Jason, you're a great communicator. That's why I think you'll be a great preacher." Then he moved on to the next person. To my knowledge, I'm the only one who even remembers that night at all.

I had no idea what he was talking about. No one had ever told me I was a great communicator before. Also, I was thirteen years old. What had I ever even communicated that was worth listening to? At least that's how I felt at the time.

He saw a gift in me that I had never seen in myself. It turns out, it's probably my greatest gift. Isn't that odd? I couldn't even see something that others thought was obvious. My friends agreed with Lowell. I was stunned.

His words were a huge encouragement to me. They were actually the words that would lead me on the path to speaking around the world and writing books. They were the challenge I needed to begin using and refining my gift. His words helped me believe in myself and pushed me to write and preach my first sermon.

Standing in Lowell's kitchen is a lot less dramatic than being suspended between the heavens and the earth on a plane built by your own sons, but the words spoken in both moments left an indelible mark on their recipients.

I have gone back to Lowell's words time and again. Especially during those defeating seasons of life that we all experience. There have been more than a few moments I wanted to give up and throw in the towel, but Lowell's words, like a faithful friend, were there to remind me what I'm capable of and who I am.

When Louie Zamperini was trying to defy the odds and succeed on the track, he nearly quit countless times. He would fondly recall in later years that it was Pete's voice and words echoing through his mind that spurred him to keep running.

I bet there are some words you fall back on too. They are a gift. It's amazing to be on the receiving end of it. But there are people in our lives who have never seen their greatest gifts and talents. They might be so obvious to us that we feel they don't need to be called out, but we must verbalize the abilities we see in others. Our words, the ones that reverberate through their thoughts when they want to give up, and our voice might just be the catalyst that propels them to new heights.

Stay In Their Ear

Much in the same way Lowell knew I was a talented communicator before I was aware of it, Moses could see Joshua's ability to lead before Joshua understood it. Moses, who famously led the people of Israel out of slavery in Egypt and on the journey to the promised land, couldn't be their leader forever. Someone had to take his place.

That someone was Joshua. One of the things I love about him is that he clearly didn't believe in himself all the time. We can all relate.

Part of Moses' job as the leader was to prepare Joshua to take his place. After Joshua led Israel's army against a neighboring enemy, God instructed Moses to memorialize the moment of Joshua's victory by writing it down. I love what God tells Moses to do next. He tells him to *recite it in Joshua's ear.*[3]

In other words, remind Joshua over and over that with God's

help he won the battle.

God told Moses to stay in Joshua's ear. The question is: why? I think it's for the same reason Orville needed to be told to go higher after he'd been flying for over six years, and I needed to hear that I was a gifted communicator more than once when I was a teenager.

We remember insults more easily than inspirations. We need the people who lead us to stay in our ear so we can get out of our own heads. Our minds can be an echo chamber for negative thoughts. We need the positive voices who speak the truth about who we are to recite it often, providing a boost to overcome the disbelief that weighs us down.

The battles with voices in our head begin early in life. My four-year-old son was having a timeout in his room, *again*. He had been acting up and needed a little time to cool off, so I gave him some.

I could hear him talking to himself over the monitor. What he was saying to himself broke my heart. He was talking about how mean of a little boy he is and that he guessed he would always be that way. I clicked off the monitor and bounded up the stairs three at a time.

When I reached his room, I took a page out of Moses' book and *got in my son's ear*. I told him that he is not a mean boy. He did a mean thing, but what he did and who he is are two very different things.

I didn't know until that moment that four-year-olds struggle with negative self-talk, but I know very well we don't quickly outgrow it. We need to be encouraged and believed in and challenged no matter how old we are. My son needed my voice at four. I needed to hear what Lowell saw in me at thirteen. Joshua needed Moses in his ear at twenty. Orville needed his dad's voice mid-flight when he was almost forty.

I love that one of Milton Wright's best moments as a father took place when he was eighty-one years old. I guess inspiring your kids and cheering them on doesn't have an expiration date. As long as there is breath in our lungs, there should be at least one voice in the ear of those we love and lead praising them for how far they've come, reciting their true identity to them, and challenging them to go higher.

Your best words can be ahead of you. Mine can be, too. There are people in our lives who need our voice. It's worth reevaluating how well we're using it. There may be a lot of noise drowning out the messages that will encourage and challenge them to reach their goals and fulfill their God-given potential. Milton didn't plan to create a memory his son would never forget, he just called out what was in his heart in the moment. Lowell wasn't trying to change my life. He just spoke what he saw in me.

Raise your voice, shout if you have to, and speak words that are the miraculous combination of challenge and encouragement. Stay in their ear. You never know when you might speak the words they will never forget.

12

Opening Move

WHEN JIM COLLINS SITS DOWN to write a book, bestsellers are a given, world-wide phenomenons are possible, becoming a classic for leaders and entrepreneurs is likely. His book *Good to Great* is on the shelf of nearly every leader I know. What intrigues me most about his storied career is the motive behind the rewrite of his first book, *Beyond Entrepreneurship*, which he co-authored with his mentor, Bill Lazier. When Bill passed away in 2004, Collins wanted to do something to honor the investment Lazier had made in his life. He rewrote the book, not only to include thirty years of research and knowledge gained since the book was first published, but he rewrote it as an act of love. Collins said he wanted to share Bill with the world. He didn't just want to share the story of how Lazier changed his life, he wanted to share Bill. I love that he said it that way. When I heard Collins explain his motivation I was hooked. I grabbed my phone and ordered the book immediately. Collins is a genius—his books are impeccably researched, filled with powerful anecdotes, and provide essential advice for business leaders—but honestly, I didn't want to learn about business; I wanted to learn about Bill.[1]

Trust

About a year after I graduated from Central Bible College in Springfield, MO, I got the opportunity to be a part of an event in the St. Louis area. In those days I wasn't pastoring a local church like I do now. I was traveling from state to state speaking at different events.

We spent the week presenting at school assemblies throughout the area that all culminated on Friday night with a huge celebration. At the assemblies, we shared a positive message with students and let them know that we were people of faith and that we'd love to tell them more at the Friday night event about how this shaped our lives. Apparently, students connected with the presentations because about three thousand rowdy teenagers showed up.

As the rookie on our speaking team, I was terrified. Graciously, my part of the routine was short. The three other guys doing it with me, Jeff, Brad, and Darin, who all had much more experience than me, did the heavy lifting. I took it as a forgone conclusion that one of them would speak at the big event that Friday. I never gave it a second thought.

So, when Jeff looked at me and told me that I would be speaking Friday night, I was shocked. I'm not sure it's medically possible to have a panic attack and pass out internally while showing no symptoms externally, but I'm fairly certain that's what happened. Jeff told me that I was the one who had a gifting from God to do this, and it was now my job. It was like a small commissioning service I hadn't known I would be attending.

To this day, I don't know what those three men saw in me or how they arrived at the conclusion that I should deliver the most important message of the entire week. Giving me that opportunity was a simple gesture, but it affected me deeply.

They trusted me.

I was blown away when they told me I would be the one speaking. It's probably the same mixture of terror and exhilaration Louie Zamperini felt when he dug his spikes into the track competing in his first major race.

Standing on the stage that Friday night, the faith that Darin, Brad, and Jeff had in me was put to the test. My thoughts were swirling as I climbed the stairs and stepped into the spotlight. I will never forget the sea of almost four hundred people that walked to the front of that massive auditorium in response to the message of hope I had shared. It was miraculous for them, and a life-changing moment for me too.

Opening Move

Before Jim Collins was a *New York Times* bestselling author of numerous books and the head of a sought-after consulting firm, he was a Stanford graduate with a lack of direction. It was then that one of his professors, Bill Lazier, gave him an opportunity he didn't feel qualified for, but changed the course of his life.

A new class was opened to make a particular course available to more students. There was only one problem: no professor had the time to teach it. Lazier stepped in and asked the school to allow a recent graduate to lead the class. If it went south, and the student failed as a professor, Lazier offered to take full responsibility.

A tenured professor at a prestigious university risked his professional reputation for a twenty-three-year-old grad student. Who does that?

When Lazier told Jim Collins he wanted him to teach the class, Collins wasn't sure he could succeed. In his mind, he was a recent graduate with no real vision for his future. He certainly didn't see himself as a professor at Stanford, but Bill Lazier did.

Collins' first attempt at teaching was a homerun. It was the first in a long line of successes. Many people teach classes, and it doesn't change their lives, but being given the opportunity to be a professor at Stanford changed Collins because it transformed how he saw himself and his potential.

Being trusted by someone we respect can reshape how we see ourselves. Being given an opportunity by them—whether we succeed or fail—shows us how *they view us.* Which, in turn, can reshape how we see ourselves.

Opening with trust has transformative power. When Bill trusted Jim with an opportunity, it reformed how he saw his own abilities. Leading with trust was one of Bill's most effective tools when championing others and helping them discover their true potential. Withholding it, on the other hand, erodes relationships from the start. Lazier knew he could get burned by giving unproven talent an opportunity, but he chose to trust in people anyway. He knew he saw something in young Jim Collins, but to convince Collins, he had to give him the chance to prove it to himself. The newly opened class was the perfect opportunity. Lazier didn't wait for Collins to earn his trust. He gave it away for free. It changed the trajectory of Collins' whole life and cemented the already close relationship the two had developed.

There were times trusting others cost Lazier. He was burned more than once, but he refused to kick the habit. A lot of people are glad he didn't. Being let down by someone is always a possibility when our opening move is trusting them. Here's the question: is it still worth it? Bill Lazier wouldn't even hesitate to affirm that it is absolutely worthwhile.

When Lazier passed away, Collins attended the funeral at Stanford's chapel expecting to be the only former student there who Lazier had impacted so powerfully. He was blown away when he arrived. The place was packed full of people that Bill Lazier had trusted with opportunities they didn't feel ready to tackle. They came to honor the man who had believed in them before they could believe in themselves.[2]

I can relate. Brad, Jeff, and Darin did the same thing for me early in my career. Their opening move was trust. I had never spoken at a major event before. The largest crowd I had ever stood before was probably a hundred people. So much effort and work had gone into the Friday night event, and if I stumbled or struggled it would be costly and it would be public. They were willing to risk their reputations and the success of the whole event to give me the chance to exercise the gifts *they* could plainly see God had given me.

That night was the moment I began to see what Lowell had seen in me and what my friends and family already knew. I was a gifted communicator.

I've had plenty of embarrassing failures as a communicator, but that night was special. The event that Friday was a huge success. I will never forget the feeling I had when I was on that stage, or the moment Darin saw me as I stepped off it. He wrapped me up in a hug and told me how proud he was of me. I sobbed. I couldn't believe how well I had done.

What I believed about myself before that week-long event was different from what I believed about myself afterward. Their trust helped me rewrite the script of what I repeatedly told myself about myself. My thoughts about my self-worth were becoming a healthier and more truthful story.

Why shouldn't I believe in myself? Jeff did. If Darin and Brad could trust me, why couldn't I trust myself? Maybe I could succeed in this new career after all. They risked an enormous amount for me that night, and it wouldn't be the last time. All of the doors that opened for me in my next season of ministry were knocked on by one of those three men. They were my biggest fans. It's not a stretch to say that because of how they championed me I've never been the same.

That is the power of trust as an opening move.

A New Name

Simon was one of Jesus' closest friends. He wasn't the best or brightest in his class, so to speak, and he hadn't gone as far in schooling as others had. He received the general education available for all boys in his day and then went back to the family fishing business instead of continuing in religious schooling. In Simon's culture, you had to be hand-picked by your teacher to continue being educated. Apparently, no one had seen that special something in Simon. Not all teachers can be Bill Lazier, I guess.

Then, along came Jesus who saw in Simon what others had overlooked. But even with Jesus championing him, Simon would be slow to grow. I can sympathize. I feel like we could be co-chairs of the slow learner's club. To help shake him out of his poor self-image, Jesus gave him a new name. He changed Simon's name to Peter—which means *the rock*.[3]

Peter was going to be a key player in establishing the foundations of the church Jesus was creating, but he wasn't there yet. There were choppy waters ahead. Giving Peter his name was an opening move of trust—a brilliant one.

We may not need a new name to get there, but everyone needs a boost along the way to believing in themselves. An opening move of trust is unrivaled in its effect on how we see our abilities and worth. We need the opportunities a mentor or friend can give that allow us to succeed or fall flat on our faces. It really doesn't matter much which way it goes.

Simon-Peter had both. His failures were spectacular. Like a belly flop off the high dive kind of spectacular. If he lived today, clips of his failures would be turned into loops and uploaded to YouTube for us to watch on repeat. Those failures came first for Peter. It was a long while before success made an appearance. Jesus' opening move had been one of trust for Peter, and despite early setbacks, he never gave up on believing in the fisherman who had been overlooked by his other teachers. Jesus knew what was in Peter. Soon, Peter, and all of us, would to.

There is an epic story at the beginning of the book of Acts. Its biblical name was the Day of Pentecost, but we can just call it the birthday of the church. Literally, this was the day that the family Jesus came to earth to establish began taking shape. However, Jesus was gone at this point. When the day arrived, and the crowd gathered, Jesus wasn't there to take the stage. I'll give you a guess as to who Jesus trusted to speak to the crowd of about three thousand. I doubt Peter was as nervous as I was.

Peter could not have felt ready for his defining role that morning, but after the dramatic events of the day and a little help from Jesus, Peter boldly took the stage and gave the speech of his life. Why shouldn't Peter believe in himself? Jesus did.

That moment set Peter up for his destiny, and it changed countless lives in the process. The audience Peter was speaking to was literally from all over the world, and they went back to their home countries sharing the same message Peter had that day, but if Jesus hadn't championed and trusted him, even after his failures, that day would have looked vastly different for Peter. He was made for that moment—Jesus just had to get him to believe he was. Because Jesus knew his potential, his opening move for Peter was trust.

I can't say for sure, but I wouldn't be surprised if speaking to the crowd that day was the first time Simon understood why Jesus had changed his name to *the rock*.

Someone Worth Trusting

I'm learning that when we are passionate about championing what God has put in others, we won't give up easily. It's one of the many things that must have made spending time with Jesus so incredible. Who doesn't want to be around a leader that believes in us more than we believe in ourselves and won't give up until we get it through our thick heads?

Some people have a strong immunity to being trusted. As we offer them opportunities, they may choose to step back instead of stepping up. The beauty is that their decision doesn't need to affect ours. Like Jesus did for Peter, we can just keep right on believing and trusting in them.

The world needs more leaders like Jesus, and Jeff, Brad, and Darin. Like Bill Lazier, too. The people who believed in me and who took a chance on me could see things that were true about me with a clarity I did not possess, and they didn't just help me understand my own potential—they taught me I can see it in others, too. I'm privileged to be part of the legacy of their leadership. As you make trust your opening move, a lot of amazing people will become a part of yours. Keep your head on a swivel with a sharp eye for the wonders woven in those around you. If they've failed before, try Jesus' method and help them back to their feet and believe in them with the same fervor as before. If you do, there will be a long list of people who discovered their destiny and came into their own because you chose to lead them with trust.

When Collins attended Lazier's funeral, he realized there were hundreds of people there that Bill had taken a chance on, and because of the book Collins wrote, people are still being impacted by Lazier's life and leadership.

Bill Lazier gave trust away like candy at a parade. He wasn't worried about his students failing, he was worried about them never trying for fear of failing. By trusting Jim Collins and countless others, Bill helped bring their potential into view. When my mentors gave me the opportunity to preach that Friday night in St Louis, they weren't just giving me a chance to prove myself; they were proving something to me—that I was someone worth trusting. Compliments are nice but they don't change our lives—opportunities do. We all need a shot to teach a class, preach a sermon, lead a meeting, or make a decision. An opening move of trust means a commitment to giving people chances. That's how we show those we're championing that we truly see and love who they are.

13

Staying Close

SCOURING THE JUDEAN COUNTRYSIDE FOR a missing animal, three Bedouin friends stumbled onto a discovery that would captivate the world.

They were tossing stones into a cave not far from the Dead Sea when they heard a strange sound. It wasn't the braying of the goat they were searching for; it was the sound of the rocks ricocheting off what turned out to be clay jars that happened to contain very ancient scrolls. The writings they discovered would become a part of a collection hidden in caves throughout the area. We know them today as the Dead Sea Scrolls.[1]

What fascinated me about this story was learning about the people who lived in the town, called Qumran, who originally wrote and preserved these scrolls. They were a community governed by strict codes who valued, above all else, purity before God. So, why did a group of people concerned about purity end up living in a remote location in the middle of the desert?

It turns out they left Jerusalem and the other populated areas because they believed everyone else was hopelessly corrupt. In their minds, they had to remove themselves from others and create a pure society unstained by the world around them. In plain English, they believed they were right and everyone else was wrong, so they moved out into the desert to wait for God to show up and vindicate them as his genuine people and then judge everyone who disagreed with them. I bet they were super fun people to have at parties.

Moving to the desert to get away from impure people is an extreme example of a mindset that is commonplace to this day:

They valued being right over relationships with others.

The people who created this little community cared about proving they were right more than anything in the world. They cut off everyone who disagreed with them and didn't want to do things their way. It's rarely a helpful approach, yet it happens frequently.

We see it all the time within families and friendships, and at the workplace too. Today, we opt for deleting people from our social media accounts rather than moving into the desert. It only requires a few clicks, and there's no sand. Double bonus. Removing people who disagree with us has never been easier.

No Retreat

Moving away from difficult people is the exact opposite of what Jesus did. He constantly moved closer to those who disagreed with him. He went into their homes and spent time with them, ate with them, listened to them, and cared for them. Jesus threw parties and hung out with people so often his detractors accused him of being a drunk. Jesus told them that if they understood who he was, they would be celebrating too. I love that.

I bet Jesus really was fun to have at parties.

One of the reasons Jesus was so great to have around is because he valued relationships over being right. He could have proved he was right from heaven. He didn't have to relinquish his throne to be right, but he did have to step down from it to have relationship with us. And that's exactly what he did.

If he had stayed comfortably seated in heaven, we wouldn't have had the chance to be loved by him, and that's what Jesus wanted more than anything. For us to experience his love.

I'm learning that when I choose being right over relationship with people I disagree with, I miss out on the chance to love them and champion them.

That's precisely what the people who wrote the Dead Sea Scrolls missed. Being the people of God meant loving a broken world, not running away from it to prove they were purer than everyone else.

It's easy to see the error when we look at an ancient community of people whose culture is so different from ours, but the mentality that led them to it is alive and well today. Unfortunately, too often, I think it's still alive a little bit in me and you.

Ruining the Vibe

My son would have loved hanging out with Jesus. Declan's favorite thing is parties. He invents get-togethers in his mind that we aren't actually planning and then gets frustrated when we tell him that we aren't having friends over on a random Thursday night.

He talks about celebrating his birthday party all year long. When he's really unhappy with us, he uninvites us to his next one by announcing, "*You're not coming to my party!*"

I want to explain to him that he wouldn't be having birthdays at all without his mother and me, but I usually let it slide.

Declan is the life of the party all the time. He's full of energy. For him, each new day is an opportunity for celebration and fun. That attitude toward life can get you into trouble with certain crowds, as it did for Jesus. It's one of the reasons we had concerns about how Declan would handle starting kindergarten. We saw danger on the horizon, and we may have prayed a time or two for extra wisdom.

When we met Declan's new kindergarten teacher just before school began, Andrea and I had one of those married couple moments where we looked at each other and communicated something without words. We both knew we were in trouble.

I'm sure his teacher was a lovely enough lady, but it was instantly noticeable that she was all about the rules. She seemed a little anti-party and kind of gave off the vibe that fun is an illness in need of a cure.

When we received an email from her after the first day of school, it was a tense moment in the Patterson house. Declan had punched a kid. On the first day! Andrea was appalled. I was, too, I guess, but I also wanted to know if he had used the technique I taught him to properly make a fist before hitting something.

Dads and moms are different, I suppose.

We got an email from her on day two as well. Not the pattern we were hoping for. She was out sick the next few days, but when she returned, so did the emails. The next one was to several parents about their kids' unacceptable behavior. She was concerned that our son, along with the other misfits, would disrupt the learning environment of her class.

Now, to be clear, we're not cool with Declan interrupting learning environments, and we work hard to teach him to be a good listener, although sometimes with questionable effect. In her emails, his teacher only talked about the rules and how he was breaking them. That bothered me. She never had one single good thing to say about my kid. It didn't sit well.

We didn't have to deal with it too long, though. Ten days into the school year, we got one final email from her. She would be retiring.

Effective immediately.

It was sudden and a little odd. I'm guessing she decided it was time to move to the desert to start a community where no one would disrupt her learning environment. I doubt we'll get invited.

Having your kid start kindergarten is a little stressful. You never know how they'll adapt. Having two teachers in the first two weeks isn't ideal either. We weren't sure how Declan's newest teacher would handle our rambunctious boy.

The contrast between his two teachers couldn't have been clearer. Several days into his second teacher's tenure, an email arrived. We thought, *here we go again.* She told us that she had noticed he was a bit energetic but that he was a delight to have in her class. She said that Declan was *right where he needs to be.*

She bought him a kick-band that attaches to the legs of his chair so that when he feels like he can't sit still anymore he can kick his feet against it. The other kids noticed, and now everyone wants one. Declan felt special.

We cried.

That phrase stuck with me. He's *right where he needs to be.* We got the distinct impression that his first teacher wished Declan wasn't in her class. I'm not accusing her of that. I'm just saying that's the vibe we got from her emails. And it made the contrast with the first email from his second teacher all the more stark.

She wasn't worried about Declan knowing the rules as much as she was concerned about him knowing he was special and welcome in her class. She valued having a relationship with my kid over the rules of the classroom. We wrote her a note and bought her a gift card. She already had a car, or we would have bought her one of those.

I think if Jesus ran a classroom, that's how everyone would feel.

Welcome and loved.

For the record, Declan's new teacher has rules for her classroom. We've since learned that she works very hard to help him understand and follow them, but she got the order correct: relationship first, rules second. We mix that up a lot. I'm not sure where she learned it, but she could have learned it from Jesus.

The most famous verse in the Bible is John 3:16. We need to read the verse that follows it, too. It says Jesus didn't come into the world to condemn everyone. Or to *prove his rules are right.* Instead, he came into the world to *save us.*

Jesus knows the rules. He made them, and they matter. In a way, his coming to earth also shows how much they matter to him. He gave his life to following them, but not just so his rules could be shown to be right. He did it so his creation could know his love.

Jesus was the master at helping outsiders, who didn't fit the mold, feel welcomed and loved. He turned misfits into insiders by inviting them to the table and keeping them close. Relationship first, rules second.

The night Jesus was arrested, he was praying in a grove of olive trees on the outskirts of Jerusalem. Before the soldiers arrived, he could have grabbed his friends who were with him and headed east over the Mount of Olives out into the Judean wilderness. He could have created a community that was purer than any the world had ever seen. It would have made those posers at Qumran look about as holy as Woodstock. But he didn't. Jesus didn't run away.

If he had, he would have missed the chance to love too many people. That's the cost of choosing being right over relationship. Jesus didn't want us to miss out on his love. It's the whole reason he came. Instead of running away from corrupt and unclean people, he ate with them, cried with them, healed them, and then died for them.

Now, he lives for them.

That's love.

No wonder God the Father gave Jesus a kingdom. He deserves one.

If we truly want to champion others there will be times we must sideline our desires to be right. As we do, our kids, classmates, co-workers, and everyone around us can discover the masterpiece God designed them to be. Fighting to prove we're right can void our influence with those we believe in most. It's not worth it. Choose relationship and stay in the fight for them to discover their God-given potential. Jesus isn't asking us to fix people, he's asking us to love and lead them by choosing relationship over being right.

Staying Close

Sometimes we push people off our team, out of our workplace, or even out of our lives. When they cause a lot of problems, we feel justified, but I wonder if often we are too quick to make that move.

I've got some tough people in my life, too. It's hard.

I've tried to get along with them, but they won't quit trying to prove they're right. It's their mission every time we're together. So, I don't invite them to every party anymore. We have to keep people close, but we also have to be wise. I have had to let some people go their own way. However, cases like this are the exception, not the rule. Sometimes I'm too quick to move those who cause me headaches and heartaches off to the side. Jesus did the opposite. He found all the difficult people and brought them close.

We all know the issues that divide us and cause disagreements. It's politics now more than ever. It's important social issues like race and equality. Even when we agree on the problems, we disagree on the solutions.

What if instead of trying to marginalize the people we disagree with, we started telling ourselves that they belong in our classrooms, on our teams, and in our families. That being close to us and at our table is right where they belong.

This is messy. Frankly, moving to the desert and focusing on purity is probably easier. Unless, of course, you want to love people and help them grow. For that, you have to get close to them and keep them there as long as possible.

I've been tasked with leading some people who gave me fits. Those assignments have caused some of the greatest pain I've experienced in life, but now, instead of quickly writing those people off, I'm trying to remind myself of something I learned from Jesus and Declan's *second* kindergarten teacher:

They're right where they need to be.

14

Show And Tell

LONG BEFORE HIS DEFINING ROLE as Obi Wan-Kenobi in *Star Wars*, famed actor Alec Guinness had a defining moment while filming *Father Brown* in rural France. During a break in the shooting, Guinness, still dressed in his costume as a Catholic priest, made the short trek to a nearby town to relax and get something to eat.

On his way back, his walk was interrupted by the voice of a young boy who shouted in French, *"Mon Père!"* *(My Father!)* Guinness had to make a split-second decision. Would he explain he was an actor in costume and not a priest? He quickly decided against it, thinking it might unsettle the little boy.

The boy clutched Guinness by the hand and quickened his pace to match a grown man's stride. Guinness decided not to speak at all since his lack of a French accent might also cause alarm. The boy swung Guinness' arm about with delight singing and chatting to himself along the way.

Then, as quickly as he appeared, the boy darted off through the hedge as they reached what Guinness assumed was his home. The role as Father Brown didn't change his career or lead to the fame he would achieve being cast in *Star Wars*, but this moment shook him inside. The boy had thought he was an actual Catholic priest. Even though he wasn't a man of faith, Guinness knew that the boy viewed a priest like a representative for God. Without speaking, without any real interaction, his mere presence as a "priest" was enough to cheer and comfort the little boy.

That simple epiphany about the power of presence would lead Guinness on the journey to faith. It was a chance encounter while on a walk, but it led to an incredible transformation in his life.[1]

We all have people in our lives who can comfort and cheer us just by being present with us. They don't even need to speak. They just have to *be with us*.

We have countless opportunities to tell people we love them; we have less chances to show them. Our presence with people is one of the most powerful ways to show people how much they matter. Being the biggest fans of those we love and lead doesn't only require well-chosen words—it demands our presence in their lives.

Tears

Spending time with Grandpa was always a boost for my soul. Listening to him tell his stories over and over quickly became a favorite pastime. One feature was always consistent during story time with him—tears. I spent a lot of mornings with Grandpa at his cottage. Without fail, he cried at breakfast telling stories. He couldn't help it. Recalling God's faithfulness moved him to tears.

The fall of 2018 was a season of tears for me. This would have been harder to admit earlier in life, but knowing Grandpa has cured me of the embarrassment of crying. During the closing months of that year, I was edging closer to a cliff and I could feel it. I was beaten down and fighting depression every day. A lot of days I felt I was losing the struggle.

This part is still a little hard to admit, but I got to the point where I just didn't want to cry alone anymore. I wanted someone to be there. So, I called up a friend to come over. Usually, when I hang out with friends we watch a football game or play golf or something. This time, he sat with me while I sobbed. I mean the ugly, uncontrollable kind of crying. If you've been there, you know what I mean. It's no picnic, but I wasn't alone and in that moment his presence meant the world to me. He didn't say anything. There wasn't anything to say. Like the little boy swinging Alec Guinness's arm, I felt comforted just by his presence.

The Bible says one of Jesus' names was *Immanuel.* It means "God with us." It fit him well. Jesus was the master at comforting people with his presence.

One of the most touching moments in his earthly life takes place in a little country town not far from Jerusalem. One of Jesus' friends, Lazarus, had died. There was a group of people at the house of Lazarus' sisters, Mary and Martha, crying with them. Literally, their job was to cry with the family and share their pain. How beautiful is that?

When she heard Jesus was calling for her, Mary ran from the

house to go meet him. Everyone jumped up and followed her because they thought she was going to go weep at the tomb of her brother. They didn't want her to cry there alone.

At first, when Mary and Martha spoke with Jesus they were upset because Jesus hadn't been with them when Lazarus was sick. They believed if he had been there, Lazarus would not have died, but in that moment, Jesus knew something that no one else did. He was about to *raise Lazarus from the dead.*

The whole reason for their pain was about to evaporate in dramatic fashion. In a few short moments, Jesus was going to trade in their sorrow for an overwhelming joy. What happened next is recorded for us in the shortest verse in the Bible:

Jesus wept.

Jesus couldn't let people cry alone. I love that about him. Why take time to cry with people who are hurting if you're about to end the reason for their suffering? Because Jesus didn't come just to heal our pain, he came to share in it with us first.

And just like Guinness, whose presence brought comfort and joy to the little boy, Jesus didn't say a word. He just wept with them.

In my darkest times, I didn't need words. I needed people to share in my pain with me and *show* me they loved me by their presence.

If we want to champion the potential of those around us, we have to learn to love them well. That means there are times we need to cry with them, rather than correct them. We need to share in their pain before attempting to fix it.

Words matter, especially the right ones in the right moment. And let's face it, Jesus knew exactly what to say to Mary and Martha in that moment. It would have been moving, I'm sure, but not as powerful as wrapping them in his strong arms and experiencing their pain with them.

The Cost

I'm one of those people who always forgets things when I pack for trips. Which I do a lot. I've flown quite a bit and worn out a lot of luggage in the process. I typically remember the essentials like socks and underwear, but toiletries seem to be left out a lot of the time. I'm not sure why I forget them. Maybe I should keep my toothbrush in my sock drawer.

What I forget most often though is the power cords for my phone and computer. If anyone who works at Apple is reading this could you make all your devices work with the same cord so I only have to remember one?

Travel used to be a big deal to me. It was a sign of success in my career as a traveling speaker. Many people think life on the road is glamorous. In the beginning, I did too. But everyone who's done it knows it's actually just tiring and uncomfortable. Somewhere along the road things changed for me. Travel wasn't about getting more speaking gigs or going to bigger and better places. It was just about being with people I love.

Paul started a number of churches around the Mediterranean world. We still have some of the letters he wrote to them. Others we've lost. In one of his writings, he told the people in the church that he longed to be with them and that he loved them with all the affection Jesus has for them.[2] I think Jesus has a lot of affection for us, so Paul really must have missed them. I'm not sure how lonely he was when he wrote it, but I can relate.

One of the places I've often visited is Ireland. I love the Irish people. They are incredibly welcoming folks. If I were writing letters on parchment like Paul, I'd address one to Dublin. The Irish people I have gotten to know over the years didn't intend to, but they changed my life. Interestingly enough, I wasn't the first person the Irish affected this way.

The Prodigal Saint

I have to confess I was more than a little disturbed the day I found out St. Patrick isn't from Ireland. I thought, *what do you mean he's not from there?* He's the embodiment of everything Irish. We paint the world green every March just to remember him. We also pinch people who don't wear green on that day, which ranks not only as odd but also a little creepy.

Patrick was British by birth, and the way he got to Ireland wasn't ideal. He didn't forget his toiletries or the cord for his laptop when he went—he never had the chance to pack at all. He was kidnapped from his home and forced into slavery. To be clear, that's not the traditional Irish welcome.

The details are foggy at this point, but we know that St. Patrick escaped his captors and made the long journey back home. That's when something odd happened. He felt God was calling him to *go back* to Ireland.

St. Patrick left the safety of home to go back to the people who enslaved him. That's a bold move. I can't imagine what moving day was like for him; packing his bags knowing he would likely never return. I bet his family wasn't too thrilled with the idea, either.

It's impossible to separate the power of his presence back in Ireland with the cost he paid to be there. He abandoned a comfortable life for a dangerous place where he faced death repeatedly. The effect of his presence is directly related to how costly it was for him to make a new home in a hostile land. No one in their right mind would do what he did, right?

But how powerful was it that he returned to the very peoples who stole his freedom? I'm sure St. Patrick told a lot of people that he loved them, and that Jesus did too. He spoke of Jesus' love in his sermons, but he illustrated it with his presence. Living among the people who had formerly enslaved him showed them the love of Jesus in a way words never could.

Jesus understood the power of presence. He knew when to speak and when to just be with those he loved, even cry with them. If we want to champion those we love the way Jesus would, then we have to master the skill of being *with* them. Not only when they are in pain, but when we are together at lunch. Being fully present by putting away our phones and being determined not to be distracted by our busy schedules is meaningful and won't go unnoticed.

I wonder what moving day was like for Jesus. What do you pack when your starting place is heaven and your destination is a dusty village on the outskirts of Jerusalem? My guess is not a whole lot. Jesus brought a lot of love and humility, but not much else.

I love the way a friend of mine says it: God's not asking us to cross an ocean, he's asking us to cross the street. It's not about our starting point or the length of our journey. It's about the destination where people we love and lead are in need of our presence in their lives.

Love was a common topic of conversation when Jesus was around. He told people their Heavenly Father loved them. Everything he did was centered around love. But he knew that telling people he loved them, or preaching sermons on love, wasn't the only way to share it. At times, it must be shown.

He paid an enormous price to be present with us. Because of its cost, his presence with us was his greatest sermon on the power of love.

It's a sermon worth repeating.

HABIT 3

Tell Them Who They Are

15

Tailored to Fit

IT IS BECOMING INCREASINGLY DIFFICULT to picture the world when people wore their best clothing every day; men in their suits and ladies in long dresses, as though weddings were announced without warning and everyone had to be ready to attend at any moment. I get uncomfortable watching movies from those time periods—everyone looks so stiff. Today, only those in the wedding actually dress up. The ladies still have beautiful dresses that are purchased and then finely tailored to fit. The men however, who no longer own suits let alone a tuxedo, rent tuxes that are *not* tailored and rarely fit comfortably. Often, they barely fit at all.

I once got a pair of tuxedo pants that were about six inches too long. It was brutal and impossible to hide. It made me look like a five-year-old wearing his big brother's pants. We used safety pins and prayer to hold them up us as best we could, but it was still noticeable to anyone within a hundred feet. My friend Josh had it even worse. His whole tux was at least three sizes too big, so it looked like he was wearing a giant trash bag. He spent a fair part of the day searching for an invisibility cloak.

As the author of Ecclesiastes famously wrote, life has its seasons.[1] Ups and downs and twists and turns are part of the journey for us all. During the most difficult times there are words we desperately long to hear. There are messages that can comfort and heal us, but we often get words spoken to us that fit about as well as Josh's tuxedo. They are well-meaning, but ineffective. We hear recycled slogans that we could have bought on a cheap piece of art at Hobby Lobby, and age-old slogans that are trotted out every time someone faces a challenge. What we need in those moments are words that fit like a finely tailored piece of clothing made to fit us and the season we're in.

Part of Us

During a difficult season in my life, I began to choose more wisely who I spent my time with. Being around life-giving people is a great way to combat life-taking situations, so it was an easy decision to spend more time with my friends Dan and Wayne, who are both incredibly upbeat people. They have known each other for a long time and have an amazing friendship. Having both planted churches themselves, they understand my journey at a deep level, too.

Dan and Wayne spoke at events together several times a year to train up people who feel called to start churches. They are amazing events, and the potential in the room is always palpable. I decided to start flying out to the events to join them. Sometimes I helped with the training in different capacities, other times I just hung out. It became a regular part of my routine every year.

After showing up for a handful of events with them, Dan and Wayne got to know me better and gain a deeper understanding of the messy season I was in. Church-planting can be hard on anyone. It was certainly getting the best of me at that point. That set Dan up for a moment I won't soon forget. We were at the airport waiting for the shuttle at the rental car return to take us to the terminal, recounting the event and how awesome it had been. We were talking about the next time he and Wayne were scheduled to speak together. I mentioned that I would definitely be coming. Dan paused, smiled knowingly, and said, "Oh, we know. We consider you to be part of us."

It was a healing message he knew I needed to hear. Finely tailored to fit me at that moment. It affected me deeply. The key for Dan was that he not only knew *who* I was, but *where* I was in that season of life. This allowed him to tailor his words to help me understand who I was not. I was *not* my loneliness. I was *not* rejected (as I often felt in that season). I was accepted and was now a part of *their friendship*. In other words, I belonged.

We can offer tailored words to others if we train our eye to see not only who they are, but what season of life they are currently in. Dan knew who I was, but he also knew the hardships of my current circumstances and my battles with loneliness.

If it were an equation it would look like this: Who + Where = Tailored Words

Armed with the knowledge of who and where people are empowers us to craft the healing messages they are longing to hear.

Anger Mismanagement

Parenting requires the skill of having the right words for our children in a wide range of situations. In their earliest years, our voices are unparalleled in shaping who they are. As every parent knows, it's a tough assignment. One I've blown many times.

During a particular season, my daughter was struggling with being frustrated and frequently angry. She kept saying, "I'm so angry," over and over. Finally, I knew it was time for a daddy-daughter talk.

Standing on a chair so our eyes could be level as she lay in her bunk bed, I told Jadice that in the Patterson household no one is allowed to say that they are angry. Side note, this is one of the best parts of adulthood. You get to make rules for your house about what people can and can't say or do. Choose wisely.

I told her that the next time she feels angry that she has to express it differently. She has to say, "I *feel* so angry." I explained the reason is simple. I told her, "You are not your emotions." She isn't her anger. It's a feeling, not an identity.

I asked her if she felt like she had a choice to be angry or not in that moment. She didn't answer. I could tell her wheels were spinning, so I explained that since it's just a feeling it's something she can control. In other words, she can choose to be angry or not. It's up to her. She doesn't *have* to be angry, because it's not who she is, it's something she feels. She doesn't have to allow her anger to be in charge.

I've had a lot of bunkbed talks that went sideways, but this was one of my better dad speeches. Those were the right words at the right moment for Jadice. They fit her like finely tailored clothes.

As we're helping those we love and lead to discover how God designed them, there will be many times we have to positively reinforce their identity and tell them who they are. For most of us, it takes a long time for those messages to truly get through. There will also be moments when we need to stop telling them who they are and start telling them who they are not.

In those seasons, declarations about where their identity is *not* rooted are words that fit like finely tailored clothes. For that bunk-bed speech knowing who my daughter was and where she was in life—struggling with anger—allowed me to tailor the words she needed to hear.

Many people in our lives think they know who they are, but their identity can easily be based on lies and half-truths. There are people who think they will always be angry, or in trouble, or out of place in the crowd. They have come to believe those negative things are *who they are.* And that they cannot change. What they will need are words that fit them well. To speak those tailored words, we have to commit to the work of seeing who and where they are.

Defining Moments

One of Jesus' closest friends had just experienced a potentially life-defining failure. Peter had betrayed Jesus and abandoned him in his greatest moment of need. Not exactly what you want on your resume if you're trying to be Jesus' disciple.

In the weeks that followed his collapse, Peter would need encouragement fine-tuned for the moment. The stakes were high. Peter was at risk of being defined for the rest of his life by his decision to publicly denounce Jesus.

In an incredible display of love and forgiveness, Jesus didn't just tailor some words for his friend, he finely crafted an entire experience. It ranks as a favorite moment of mine in the Bible.

Peter's epic blunder happened the day Jesus was arrested. Late that night, while Jesus was being run through a series of trials where the verdicts were decided before the proceedings began, Peter was out in the courtyard quietly waiting in the cool evening air. As he joined a little group of people warming themselves around a small charcoal fire, he was recognized as a friend of Jesus. Peter denied it, bitterly and repeatedly. After the third time he swore he didn't know Jesus, he ran out into the street and collapsed into a pile on the cobbled stones. Peter lost it. It was probably an ugly cry, close to wailing. He couldn't believe what he had done.

It had only been hours earlier that he promised Jesus, to his face, that he would *never* turn away from him even if it cost him his life. Jesus knew Peter was headed for trouble and told him that when the time came, Peter wouldn't make good on his promise.

It's important to pause and make sure we all catch that part of the story. Jesus *knew* Peter wasn't going to keep his promise. It makes what Jesus does for Peter all the more moving.

Not long after Peter's denial, Jesus was raised from the dead. Their friend was alive again, but Peter and the other disciples still didn't know what was next. They didn't know what they were supposed to do yet, so they went back to their homes and to their former careers. Peter and several others climbed back in their boats and began to fish again.

After a night of casting their nets with no luck, Jesus came to the banks of the water to meet them. Standing in the boat within earshot of shore, Peter realized it was Jesus that had come to see them. He lept from the boat and swam to him.

Wading out of the water Peter discovered a scene that had been carefully orchestrated by Jesus. Over a charcoal fire, Jesus was cooking breakfast for the small group of friends. Let that sink in. The resurrected Lord of the whole world was *making breakfast* for his friends. The next time you think you can't change the world as a stay-at-home parent or as someone's friend, remember this moment between Jesus and Peter. To make a difference you don't need a stage, just a skillet.

There are only two times in the entire Bible that a fire is specifically said to have been kindled by charcoal. The first is when Peter was warming his hands while denying Jesus; the other is this moment.[2] While they were eating, Jesus then asked three times if Peter loves him. Once for each of the times Peter denied him. Every detail was tailored to fit.[3]

Jesus recreated the circumstances of Peter's denial with great care and purpose. The question is, why?

I think it's because Peter needed to hear who he was *not*. He was not his broken promise to Jesus. He was not his failures. He was still Jesus' follower and friend.

Jesus was there that morning to make sure Peter knew it.

It wasn't only tailored words; it was a finely tailored experience. It was exactly what Peter needed and it changed the trajectory of his life. If Jesus hadn't recreated the scene of the fateful night of Peter's failure, it could have defined him for life. The pain of his broken promise was a bitter mistake. I wonder how many times he replayed the scene later in life. My guess is a lot, but each time he did he had this breakfast with Jesus to counter its influence over him.

We must tailor moments and messages for those we love and lead. The risk of them being defined by their mistakes and failures is too high. We have the ability to do what Jesus did for Peter by creating moments that will help them heal, shape how they think about themselves, and counter the lies that could define them. We can help them shape the truths they need to speak over their own lives: *I am not my anger, my past, or my addictions. I am not my failures, my faults, or my broken promises.*

Make It Fit

When we tailor-make words for people that they need to hear, we give them something of value to keep. They can repeat the life-giving things we have spoken over them in their minds again and again. It's like a check they can cash over and over when the resources they need to fight their battles are depleted.

Tailoring words and creating moments for those we love and lead isn't always easy, but it's always worth it. Even if it costs us a little time and energy. I have a friend who once drove eight hours to give his brother a hug just because he knew he needed one. It feels like something Jesus would do. His brother was really struggling during that season of his life. Each time he messed up, the weight and the memories of all his past failures would come crashing down on him again, so while he was there, he told his brother something he knew he needed to hear: *You are not your failures.* They both broke down in tears. It didn't fix everything overnight, but it gave his brother a moment he could use to fight the lies that might otherwise define him.

There are powerful messages people around us need to hear. How we deliver those messages matters because a compliment or piece of encouragement doesn't land the same on every person. A suit isn't great because the fabric is nice or because the buttons are fancy. A suit is great because it fits you perfectly. A tailor measures your chest, arms, waist, and inseam. He asks you where you want your pants to hit and how much shirt sleeve you want to peek out of your jacket. It fits you because it was made for you, and only you.

Our words should be like finely tailored clothing. It's less about the material and more about the fit.

Find those in your life who you love and lead. Pull them over, pick them up, and tell them who they are or who they are not. Like Dan's words to me or the breakfast Jesus made for Peter, it may crack open the door to a new wave of healing and hope. Drive eight

16

One More Lap

PRECISELY AT 8:32 AM ON July 16, 1969, three rockets each the size of a Navy destroyer roared to life creating a thrust that would send three US astronauts to the moon. The enormous Saturn V rockets burned through a swimming pool's worth of fuel every four seconds during the initial launch phase. I suppose I should stop complaining about the gas mileage my truck gets.

These rockets, and the 750,000 gallons of fuel they contained, were used only for the first stage of the flight. Two minutes and forty-four seconds after launch, at an altitude of 120 miles and a speed over 17,000 mph, two of the Saturn V's rockets were released, and the spacecraft entered its second stage of flight: one lap around the Earth.

It took about ninety minutes.

It takes us longer to do a load of laundry. Unless you're one of those people like me, who puts everything on the speed cycle because we assume our clothes can't be *that* dirty.

The astronauts of the Apollo 11 mission needed the speed to

achieve escape velocity. At 17,000 mph, they were still about 8,000 mph shy of what it takes to leave the Earth's gravitational pull and fly to the moon.

It took one more lap around the Earth and a quick burn of the single remaining Saturn V rocket at the last moment to reach 24,791 mph and fly into outer space. That's fifty times the cruising speed of a Boeing 747 and well in excess of one hundred times the top speed of the fastest racing cars ever built. Without this extra lap, the Apollo 11 mission wouldn't have had the momentum to reach outer space, let alone the moon.

We are all trying to generate the necessary momentum to achieve our ambitions. We love reaching the next goal, completing the next project, or winning another victory. The thing is, our next move shouldn't be to rush into a new ambition. First, we need to circle what was just accomplished one more time. That's what will create the best momentum for us to move toward our goal. It is one of our best opportunities to champion people by celebrating who they are and what they've done. Speeding off to the next goal will force us to fly by one of our best opportunities to champion those we love.

Autopilot

I'm the kind of guy who's always ready to move on to the next big thing. I rarely stop to look back at what was just achieved. I barely even think about it. After accomplishing one goal, I immediately move on to the next. Dreaming is my autopilot. I do it without thinking.

Every year on the anniversary of the grand opening of our church we have a dinner party for our staff and key leaders, which we call our leadership family. The reason for the party is to celebrate the previous year and cast a vision for where we're heading. Because of my wiring, the celebration of the past usually takes about ten minutes, and then I'm headed toward the future as fast as possible.

In my excitement to land our team on the moon, I forget to circle the earth one more time. Skipping the final lap may not make our dreams impossible like it would have for the Apollo 11 crew, but I'm learning there is a cost, especially over time. It burns people out and causes others to feel overlooked and underappreciated. To truly champion people we have to motivate them toward growth. Failing to take one more lap to recognize their accomplishments demotivates them, stunts their development, and can eventually negate the influence we had in their lives.

Mercifully, I only led this meeting twice before I turned it over to John. Early in the life of our organization, I made a welcome discovery: John had kept a record of all the fantastic things that had happened throughout the year. No one had asked him to do it. He just did it. It's John's autopilot.

Keeping a record of the amazing accomplishments of those around me isn't an idea I would have come up with in ten lifetimes, probably. Paul, in a letter to some friends who had gotten a little off track, said that love keeps no record of wrongs, but I'd be far more likely to make that kind of list or at least keep track of things people did that annoyed me. I'm a perfectionist, prone to noticing even tiny things that are wrong, like someone not pushing in their chair after getting up. I know, I know, I'm asking Jesus to help me. Now, I'm discovering from friends who are wired differently than me that racing toward future dreams isn't necessarily the best approach or even the fastest way to get there.

The best way to accomplish our ambitions, to lead our teams toward growth, to help our loved ones discover their potential is to take the final lap. Keep records of what they do right, even the little things, and celebrate them like crazy. That's what being someone's champion truly looks like. If you want to help them discover the wonders God has woven into them, take one more lap.

Remembering Ebenezer

As the legend goes, Ebenezer Lennox Scroggie was a nineteenth-century Scottish merchant of wine and corn. Known for his fun-loving demeanor, the wild parties he threw for guests, and a bit of an irreverent attitude toward the church, Scroggie was the guy to have around. By all accounts, he was a successful and generous business-man.[1] Perhaps his greatest claim to fame was winning a contract to cater food for the visit of George IV to Edinburgh in 1822 and the first contract to provide the Royal Navy with whiskey. Hopefully, someone else had the contracts for the other necessary items like fuel and ammunition.

One day in 1841, the legacy of Scroggie's life changed forever when the caption on his gravestone, which read "meal man," was misread as "mean man" by a passerby who was having a momentary bout of dyslexia, named Charles Dickens. Killing time before an event he was scheduled to speak at in Edinburgh, Dickens took a stroll through the Canongate Kirk graveyard and forever misrepresented Scroggie's life by naming the most iconic character of his literary career after him.[2]

Following the publication of Dickens' A Christmas Carol in 1843, the name Ebenezer unsurprisingly fell out of favor with parents as a name for their baby boys. A cold heart and penny-pinching habits led to the name Ebenezer Scrooge becoming synonymous with the word miser.[3]

Like the Apollo 11 astronauts, Dickens needed to circle that tombstone one more time. I wonder what might have happened if he had taken a longer look that day?

What other things might we miss when we forget to take one more lap?

I have come to believe that when you have a team member who does something well on autopilot, let them do it. So, despite my reservations about letting go of leading the most important meeting of the year, I put John in charge. With John at the helm, the celebration of our team—both what they have accomplished, and who they are as individuals—is the first ninety minutes of the meeting instead of the first ten. It's our all-important lap around the earth. It sets the trajectory and builds the necessary momentum for the next twelve months. My vision for the future is now the final ten minutes. It sets our coordinates. It's no longer the fuel for the trip.

John, in another flash of brilliance, named the annual celebra-

tion our *Ebenezer Night*. The name Ebenezer has biblical roots that
stretch well beyond Dickens all the way back to 1 Samuel. After a
victory against a neighboring people, Samuel set up a stone as a
memorial, named it Ebenezer, and said up until that point God had
helped them. No matter what may lie ahead, Samuel was saying that
he would choose to remember and celebrate what God had done.[4]

Our Ebenezer Night serves as a final lap around the previous
year and builds momentum for the year to come for our leaders.
One more lap around Earth propelled the astronauts to where they
were going, but one more lap around our friend's lives will help
them grow into who they're becoming.

Celebrate people by making one more lap around them. Whether you lead an organization or not, opportunities to be someone's
biggest fan abound. Remind them about the moments when they
were brave and courageous. Buy them lunch to celebrate their
promotion. Tell them how much growth you've seen in their lives
recently. Whether we're leading our team at home, at the office, or
on the field, the fix is to take extra laps, celebrate more wins along
the way, and appreciate the contributions others have made.

Labels

My wife, Andrea, and I are blessed with three sweet children who fill
our home with joy and so many messes. After his first day at a
summer camp put on by a local church, one of the teachers said of
my son, Declan, "He's a ball of energy!" That's putting it mildly. A
more apt description would be he's like Sonic the Hedgehog on Red

ONE MORE LAP 179

Bull. Tiring him out every day requires creativity. He's also genuinely the most tender-hearted little boy I've ever known. One night I tucked him in bed before leaving for a short trip. When I told him I would be gone before he woke up the following day, he sat up in bed, wrapped his little arms around my neck, and whispered in my ear, "I'll miss you, daddy." I nearly canceled my flight on the spot.

Our street is a quiet little cul-de-sac shared with ten neighbors. People frequently walk with their kids or dogs up and down the street. One evening Andrea was walking the kids past one of our neighbors, who happened to be sitting near the end of his driveway. He pointed at Declan and said, "That one's a little terror."

Andrea's first emotion was anger. Which was followed by the thought, how dare he label my little boy with something like that? When I heard what he had said, my first thought was to chisel "mean neighbor" onto his tombstone someday. I'm probably not that bold, so maybe I'll settle for "meal neighbor" and wait for a dyslexic passerby to decode it.

We are given labels all the time in life. Often, it's not by grumpy neighbors who somehow have never come to understand that words have power. Unfortunately, too often those labels aren't given by neighbors and strangers, they are given by people who should have loved us and been our biggest fans. When this happens, those negative words continue taking laps around us, empowering a false narrative about who we are. Many of us wouldn't think to keep a list of amazing things about those we love and lead, but without intentionality on our part, the words that echo in the minds of others can be all the wrong ones—with catastrophic effect.

Dickens wrote in his journal the day he passed by Scroggie's grave that the phrase "mean man" etched on his tombstone must have been a "terrible burden" to carry into eternity with him. It was actually a terrible weight that Dickens placed on him.

Words have the power of life and death. They can put labels on us that are heavy burdens to bear. Sometimes we carry them for life. That's why Andrea was so upset that our neighbor would say something like that. He doesn't even know Declan. At least Dickens waited until Scroggie was dead.

Even when spoken without devastating intent, words can cause damage. One author said the tongue is like a small flame that sets a whole forest ablaze. His name was James; he was the half-brother of Jesus. I hope he had a good therapist after growing up with a perfect sibling, but even being perfect, people still tried to label Jesus with all sorts of things that weren't true or kind.

I'd love to judge my neighbor more. No, really, I would. But how often do I do the same thing to people around me, even people I love, with careless words? I can be prone to forgetting how powerful my words can be. We all can.

I'm learning that sharing words with positive power takes more work for me. I want to have a better vision for the people around me that I lead and love, but I have to learn to slow down and take one more lap around who they are and what they've accomplished. One of the best ways to champion people is to celebrate them well and call out the good we see in them. This habit can keep us from the careless words that label others and burden them with false perceptions of who they really are. We can't champion people effectively if we don't steward our words well.

Failing to remember and celebrate others and what they've done can lead to a false perception of who they are—remembering the wrong rather than the right, making it difficult to be their biggest fan. At the end of Dickens' tale, Scrooge is a repentant sinner and a changed man, but his name isn't synonymous with turning your life around. No one calls a person fresh out of rehab a Scrooge even though it might be appropriate in Dickens' mind at least. One more lap around Scroggie's grave may have corrected the false perception Dickens developed about him. One more lap around those we love and lead can do the same for us. Extra laps help us to see their true worth and the wonders Jesus has woven into them.

We're in danger of misrepresenting people's lives all the time by keeping a record of all the wrong things. If my friend John is awake, he's celebrating something or someone. It will take me a few more laps to get there, but I'm so much farther along than I used to be. The people I love and lead are better off for it. I bet you can make some progress too. When you do, let me know—I'll take a lap with you, and we'll celebrate like crazy!

One More Lap

The shortest distance between two points is always a straight line, but it's not always a path we can travel if we want to reach our destination. If the Apollo 11 crew would have headed straight for the moon, they would have saved ninety minutes. They also never would have landed there. They would have come up more than 238,000 miles short of their target. While their extra lap used up time and valuable fuel, it wasn't a detour or a hold up—it was a planned part of the mission. It didn't guarantee they would survive the rest of their journey into uncharted territory, but it made it possible.

What if we planned some more laps? And started keeping a record of wins for people in our lives and celebrated them without warning? How might it change our organizations, our lives at home, or how our kids and friends understand their worth and value? It will take effort from those of us who don't do this on autopilot, which I'm guessing is most of us. Hopefully, it won't take swimming pools worth of fuel to launch us into this habit, but just because it's not our first nature doesn't mean it can't become second nature.

It may seem like these extra laps of celebration could slow down all the dreams I'm living for, but I'm realizing more and more that it's not only the fastest way to achieve my goals; it's also the most enjoyable. I'm slowly learning to take the last lap, to throw parties like my friend John, and live by a simple maxim:

Celebrate everyone and everything.

Epilogue

THESE DAYS, I'M TAKING FEWER laps around my pain and a lot more around my friends. It's been a process, but I've made a lot of progress. You can too. I don't know what you're circling in your life, but I know you can begin to make it those you love and lead.

It's easy to read a book like this and still not know exactly where to start. I'd say, start by championing the person right in front of you.

Every time I resolve to read Scripture more, I find myself wanting to get a new Bible, as though the reason I don't read the copy I currently have is because it's too old. It's a ridiculous notion that getting a new Bible will actually make me more apt to read it, but I still feel that way. The same feelings can arise when it comes to discovering the potential in others. We can slip into the mentality that as soon as we find some new people, we'll champion them, when the truth is, all we need to do is believe in those around us. We don't need new people any more than I needed a new Bible.

Since you've made it to the epilogue, I'm gussing you've adopted the mentality we began with: we are all God's masterpiece. I'm so glad you did. I think Jesus is bursting with joy because of that decision. Your insecurity and ego—along with a host of other obstacles—will keep getting in the way. Just keep putting that version of yourself on the bus with a one way ticket out of town. Eventually, your old self will show up less and less. It'll be a process, but if you keep Jesus close you'll make it through.

Find someone today and ask them some great questions. Learn about who they are, figure out how to love them better, and tell them the beautiful things you see in them as often as possible. There will be times you have to speak the truth in love about some not-so-beautiful things. Just make sure that on balance there is far more of the former than the latter.

I'm happy to report that my mother-in-law, Ann Mainse, is now cancer free! She wrote an amazing devotional book about her experiences with Jesus while on her journey with cancer. You can pick it up at Amazon. It's called, *Coffee with Him: Mornings with God on an Unexpected Journey.*

If you're wondering what happened to the poor guy I unloaded on for two-hours while circling a shopping center, he's still on our team. In fact, he's our Executive Pastor now. Thank God for grace and forgiving friends.

Our church has seen a lot of amazing things happen while learning to champion those around us. We recently started a new routine: each December, we require everyone in our leadership family to turn in a dream they want to accomplish for the upcoming year (we got the idea from an executive at Chick-fil-A!). There's only one rule: the dream can't be anything related to their work at the church!

It has to be a personal dream that we can champion and celebrate.

Some staff members have started successful businesses. Others have gotten their Master's Degree, read more books, taken trips to see people they love more often, and a whole host of other worthwhile endeavors. One person fulfilled a dream and read through the entire Bible. He didn't even have to buy a new one!

Our children's pastor, Stacy Nuttall, set a goal to run a half-marathon with her sister. Due to a continuing battle with an illness, her sister couldn't make it, so our staff and their spouses divided up the race into sections and ran it with her. It was a blast, and it led to a new rule for our team: no one ever runs alone.

There are some people near you who are running their race alone and are desperately in need of someone to run with them, encourage them, and celebrate their progress in life. Get out of the stands and into the race. Be the biggest fan of those you love and lead!

Acknowledgements

IT WOULD BE IMPOSSIBLE TO write a book that includes all the people who have believed in me and been my biggest fans. To all those whose names do not appear in these pages, I want to offer sincere thanks. I am deeply in your debt for your support throughout the years.

To Andrea, Jadice, Declan, and Rowan, my heartfelt thanks for the sacrifices you made while I was working on this project. More than a few evenings and Saturdays were spent without my presence at home to make this possible. I am your biggest fan. Thanks for being mine. Your love and encouragement are the only reason I accomplish anything. I love you all so much.

Thank you to Bob Goff and Kim Stuart. This book never would have happened without your friendship. From the beginning of the process, you told me we were a team. It felt that way every step of the journey. Your tireless encouragement and input were indispensable to me. Setting out to write my first book was daunting. You believed in me before I believed in myself. I'll never forget it. I've always said that if I were going to write a book, I wanted to have a great team, and you were better than I ever could have hoped for or imagined.

John Baughman, thanks for being an incredible friend who was willing to read the roughest drafts of these chapters. You understood what I was trying to accomplish with this book and your thoughts and insights were spot on. As always, your encouragement was invaluable. You're not only one of my biggest fans, but one of my best friends. You make me better in every way.

Thanks to my editor, Allie Baughman. I am deeply in your debt. Your keen eye and brilliant mind were exactly what was needed to help me stay on message in each chapter and throughout the book. Anything this book lacks, is entirely my fault. To the final member of the Baughman family, Charlie, I love you buddy. You're too young to help with the book, but your smile always makes my day.

To the staff at Parkside: Allison, Stacy, Nii, Anna, and Andrew, thank you all for how hard you work and how much you love our church. Without your support and the slack you picked up while I was writing, this book wouldn't have been possible. Thanks for being patient with me while I try to figure out how to better be your biggest fan. I love you all.

Pastoring at Parkside has been one of the greatest joys of my life. To my church family, you all are the reason I love it so much. I cannot believe God has given me the opportunity to be in your lives. I cannot wait to see what God has in store for us in the future.

One of the best leaders I know has somehow always flown under the radar. Andy, I hope this book shows our peers what hundreds of students at Missouri State Chi Alpha have always known: you are not only an amazing friend but a remarkable leader.

I love the cover of this book. Todd, thanks for jumping in at a moment's notice and doing what you always do: come up with something creative and perfect. Thanks for being a co-conspirator for all of my projects, past and future.

To all my friends at The Oaks, it has been a joy to get to know you all while writing this book. You have made me feel like part of the family there. Thanks so much for your hospitality and friendship.

To my parents, your support and prayers paved the road for everything I have accomplished. I love you.

Finally, to Grandpa, thank you for being my hero, my biggest fan, and my friend. I love you. I miss you and your voice in my life so much.

Resources at biggestfanleaders.com

One More Lap Journal

Most of us aren't wired like my friend John; we need a primer to start writing down the accomplishments and wins of those we love and lead, but this is as good a time as any to create the habit.

Don't just record the big wins, throw in the little ones too. Invite someone to lunch, throw a party, or get your team together and celebrate all the progress you've made together. You can even call it Ebenezer night if you want. Celebrating people well is essential, but it's not automatic. It will take discipline and planning. Grab a *One More Lap Journal* and start writing down reasons to celebrate with those around you.

From Your Biggest Fan Cards

Keep turning champion into a verb by celebrating the people in your life. We created some cards for people in our organization to share what they love about others. We call them biggest fan cards. On the front it says, "From Your Biggest Fan." It's an easy way to make a meaningful little lap around someone's life. It won't even take you ninety minutes.

Believing the best about others and telling them what we see in them doesn't have to be complicated. I'll bet you could write a couple notes like this today and shock your best friend, a co-worker, or your kids. If you're married, I humbly suggest starting with your spouse. My friend Nate got inspired with this idea and asked me for a pile of biggest fan cards. He wrote notes to all one hundred seventy-nine of his tenth-grade students at the end of the school year.

You don't need official stationery. Any spare paper, even a text message, and a little bit of reflection about someone and some appreciation for who they are and what they mean to you is enough, but if you want the official cards you can pick them up at our website.

Notes

Part I: A New Mindset

1. "George Bernard Shaw Quotes", BrainyQuote.com. BrainyMedia Inc, 2022. Accessed Jan. 29, 2022. www.brainyquote.com/quotes/george_bernard_shaw_386923

Chapter 1: The Fastest Man Alive

1. Laura Hillenbrand, *Unbroken* (New York: Random House, 2010), 13-15.

2. Hillenbrand, *Unbroken*, 15, 17-28, 43-45.

3. Hillenbrand, *Unbroken*, 8. Reading the sentence referenced here about Louie being the slowest kid in town changed my life. I stopped reading the book as it dawned on me that all this incredible potential was in Louie, but early in his life no one could see it. God helped me realize this is true of every person. That sentence is the catalyst God used for me launch our church, and eventually write this book!

4. "This is What We'll See When Betelgeuse Really Does God Supernova", *Forbes*, Jan. 23, 2020, www.forbes.com/sites/startswithabang/2020/01/23/this-is-what-well-see-when-betelgeuse-really-does-go-supernova

5. "Light Pollution", *International Dark Sky Association*, www.darksky.org/light-pollution

6. Ephesians 2:10, New Living Translation.

Chapter 2: The Ripple Effect

1. David Rubenstein, *American Story: Conversations with Master Historians*, Audible, 2019. Audiobook.

2. Bob Goff, *Shifting Your Perspective*, Dream Big Podcast, April 14, 2021, www.accessmore.com/episode/Michael-Jr---Shifting-Your-Perspective

Chapter 3: Vision for People

1. Daniel James Brown, *The Boys in the Boat: Nine Americans and Their Epic Quest for Gold at the 1936 Berlin Olympics* (New York: Viking, 2013), 334-335, 346.

2. Brown, *Boys in the Boat*, 346-350.

3. Brown, *Boys in the Boat*, 350.

Part II: The Obstacles in our Path

1. "Albert Einstein", AZQuotes.com. Win and Fly LTC, 2022. Accessed Jan. 29, 2022. www.azquotes.com/quote/522352

Chapter 4: 10,000 Episodes

1. The pastor who said this was Craig Groeschel. It was in the the episode he interviewed Bob Goff. You can find the link in the notes for chapter seven.

2. "World's Columbian Exhibition", *Wikipedia*,
   en.wikipedia.org/wiki/World%27s_Columbian_Exposition

3. Mark 10:45.

Chapter 5: Give Credit Away

1. "Benjamin G. Lamme", *Wikipedia*,
   en.wikipedia.org/wiki/Benjamin_G._Lamme

2. Mark Bussler, dir., *Westinghouse: The Life and Times of an American Icon*, 2010, www.amazon.com/Westinghouse-Life-Times-American-Icon/dp/B004SAU12U

3. "Edison & Tesla", 2016, edison.rutgers.edu/tesla.htm

Chapter 6: The Pain Scale

1. Michael Rossi, dir., *Mr. Tornado* (PBS, 2020).
   www.pbs.org/wgbh/americanexperience/films/mr-tornado

2. "*Hell Week*", navyseals.com/nsw/hell-week-0

Chapter 7: Moonshot

1. "*Our Manifesto*", accessed June 18, 2021, national.cc/about/ncc-manifesto

2. Craig Groeschel, *Becoming an Authentic Leader*, Craig Groeschel Leadership Podcast, Jan. 17, 2019,
   www.youtube.com/watch?v=FlBOUqpHeH0

Chapter 8: Choose Positivity

1. Ryen Russillo, *How Marvel Changed the Movie Industry with Ben Fritz and Professional Life Advice with Trevor Moawad*, The Ryen Russillo Podcast, podcasts.apple.com/gb/podcast/the-ryen-russillo-podcast/id1433966613?i=1000495517005

2. Luke Ellis and Bruce Nash, *Modern Marvels: Machu Picchu*, Sept. 24, 2003, www.youtube.com/watch?v=bZdELQOmap4

3. Tom Rath and Donold O. Clifton, *How Full Is Your Bucket*, (New York: Gallup Press, 2015), 7-9.

Part III: The Way Forward

1. "Jim Ryun Quotes", BrainyQuote.com. BrainyMedia Inc, 2022. Jan. 19, 2022. www.brainyquote.com/quotes/jim_ryun_127356

Chapter 9: The Journalist Mindset

1. Jedd Medefind and Eric Lokkesmoe, *Revolutionary Communicator: Seven Principles Jesus Lived to Impact, Connect, and Lead*, (Winter Park: Relevant Books, 2004), 2.

2. Mark 10:46-52.

Chapter 10: Friend

1. Margaret Grossi, dir., *The Boys of '36*, Aug. 1, 2017, www.pbs.org/wgbh/americanexperience/films/boys36/#film_description

    This quote is recounted by Joe Rantz's daughter, Judy Willman, during an interview. Decades after these events she still became emotional telling her father's story.

2. John 15:12-17.

3. Luke 5:27-32.

Chapter 11: Higher!

1. "Milton Wright (bishop)", Jan. 19, 2022,
    en.wikipedia.org/wiki/Milton_Wright_(bishop)

2. The sign commemorating this moment can be found at Huffman Prarie
    on the walking path the follows the flight path the Wright brothers took
    on their flights.

3. Exodus 17:14, ESV.

Chapter 12: Opening Move

1. Brené Brown, *Curiosity, Generosity, and the Hedgehog with Jim Collins*,
    Dare to Lead Podcast, Dec. 14, 2020, brenebrown.com/podcast/brene-
    with-jim-collins-on-curiosity-generosity-and-the-hedgehog

2. Brené Brown, *Jim Collins*.

3. Matthew 16:18.

Chapter 13: Moving to the Desert

1. "*The Dead Sea Scrolls*", Sept. 11, 2017,
    www.museumofthebible.org/book-minute/the-dead-sea-scrolls?

Chapter 14: Show and Tell

1. Alec Guinness, *Blessings In Disguise*, (New York: Knopf, 1986).

2. Philippians 1:8.

Chapter 15: Tailored to Fit

1. Ecclesiastes 3:1-8.

2. See John 18:18, and John 21:9.

3. John 21:1-19.

Chapter 16: One More Lap

1. *"A Life Wasted: Who Was the Real Ebenezer Scrooge,"* Dec. 11, 2021, www.bbc.co.uk/programmes/articles/4y78YB9vVMG1xYrW8CmzjPw

2. *"How an Edinburgh Gravestone Inspired Ebenezer Scrooge,"* De. 14, 2016, www.edinburghnews.scotsman.com/whats-on/arts-and-entertainment/how-edinburgh-gravestone-inspired-ebenezer-scrooge-609726

3. *"Revealed: The Scot Who Inspired Dickens' Scrooge,"* Dec. 24, 2004, www.scotsman.com/news/revealed-scot-who-inspired-dickens-scrooge-2470097

4. 1 Samuel 7:12.

About the Author

Jason Patterson serves as the Lead Pastor of Parkside Church in Fishers, IN. He and his wife, Andrea, moved to the Indianapolis area near the end of 2015 with a team of people to start a church known for its radical compassion and generosity.

Prior to starting the church Jason traveled widely for over fourteen years speaking at churches and events. He has spoken to hundreds of thousands of people across the US and around the world. If you are interested in booking Jason for your church or event, you can visit www.jasonmpatterson.org.

Jason also does coaching for church and business leaders. If you are interested in coaching, you can get more information at www.biggestfanleaders.com/coaching.

Discussion Questions

Looking to go deeper? Questions are available for your use personally or within a small group. You can download a PDF by visiting:

www.biggestfanleaders.com/questions

9 781957 690032